→DO I←

CONTRADICT

MYSELF?

VERY WELL, THEN,

I CONTRADICT MYSELF;

I AM LARGE—

I CONTAIN

MULTITUDES.

- WALT WHITMAN

Acknowledgements

One of the gifts of working in healthcare is that you are constantly surrounded by people who invest their careers, their time and their passions in helping people live healthier lives. They are obsessed with how to create change. As a close colleague once said, they "never stop flying the airplane," always looking for a new way to motivate and connect with people.

Their work inspires our work as we watch them make powerful impacts on lives and health, simply by focusing on what people most need to succeed.

We owe particular gratitude to our closest partners and fellow researchers, including **Jeff Brodscholl, Ph.D.** (behavioral science), **Linda Adams Matanovic** and **Joe Immen** (book design), **Benjamin Abramowitz** (editor), **Carolyn Stephenson** (insights), **Alex Brock** (insights), **Baba Shetty** and **Amy Hutnik** (collaborators).

All proceeds from this book will be donated to The STARR Coalition, a nonprofit organization working to bring together thought leaders within clinical research, pharma and advocacy.

Contents

Introduction

Why do you do the right things for your health? Is it because you want to meet a doctor's expectations? Because you want to finally succeed at that diet and exercise plan? Or just simply because you want to feel in control?

Most of our healthcare environment is built around commands and promises: *this is what you should do* or *this is what I will do*. But that approach gets people caught up in a cycle of credit and debit behavior that's hard to get out of. One small win is followed by a small miss or an everyday failure that leads to guilt and apathy, sapping motivation to continue. If you ever try at all, that is.

Success is a one-time measure. The ability to keep going, to succeed again and again, and ultimately meet those healthcare intentions—that's about motivation and resilience.

Yet the ability to help people stay motivated is often lost in healthcare communications that aren't connected to how people actually make decisions and change their behavior.

So, how do we motivate people? How do we give them the resilience to try and then try again?

Our industry and our world are fascinated by that question right now. We've seen a rapid expansion of our understanding of human behavior driven by new insights from the behavioral and social sciences – disciplines including behavioral economics, psychology, and neuroscience are all adding to this collective knowledge base. That new understanding is landing on consumer bookshelves, favorite podcasts and major television programs. Of course it is: because we all want to know *why* people do what they do.

Healthcare was among the first realms to nurture this curiosity about how to help people realize the change they want for themselves. The industry has piloted evidenced-based nudges and other programs designed to influence choices and behaviors. Papers have been written on the small-population impact of those programs, pointing to incredibly compelling opportunities to scale.

And, yet, despite the new knowledge, the compelling experiments, and the momentary *ah-has*, healthcare advocates, professionals and companies still communicate and behave in counterintuitive ways that impact both the topline of patient health and the bottomline of sector growth.

Why do many of our organizations and colleagues continue to communicate healthcare information in ways that are outdated and unexamined? Maybe because behavioral science is – at its core – science. It's big, complex and interconnected. Most healthcare professionals and communicators receive it bit by bit. A headline here, a presentation there. They don't have a comprehensive view into how to make relevant connections to their own objectives. That bit-by-bit science might look interesting but not be actionable. Or, it might lead to experiments with one well-publicized model and leave more relevant approaches on the table.

What would healthcare innovation look like if stakeholders had that comprehensive view and felt well equipped to use evidence-based levers of change in every communication or customer solution?

In this book, we teamed up a behavioral scientist and a healthcare communicator to work together to create one clear picture of what we know and how we can apply it in the everyday work of helping more people live healthier lives.

First, let's agree, this is hard work.

Adding behavioral science to existing healthcare communications or solutions introduces a new, challenging piece to the puzzle. It will require you and your team to think about every aspect of your current communications and solutions in new ways. To give old puzzle pieces new roles and learn how to put all the pieces together for each patient and healthcare stakeholder.

Jason Choi, the Science Department Chair at a New York high school called Sleepy Hollow, explained that kind of interruptive thinking to his students with a simple tangram puzzle.[1] Want to try it?

✂ Start by cutting out these five pieces from his experiment:

Set the small square aside. ⟶

Now, try to build a square with the remaining four pieces.

Most people can build that puzzle pretty quickly, in just a few minutes.

Now, add that small square back into the mix. Can you remake the puzzle with that one additional piece? Solved correctly, it will still make the same shape.

You can see the solution to both puzzles on **pages 126-127.**

Reprinted with kind permission from Jason Choi.

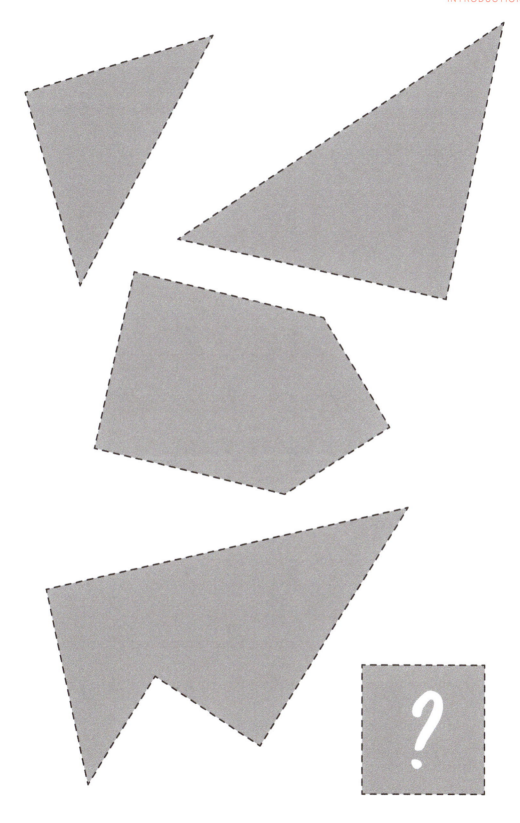

Did that second puzzle take a lot longer? Of course it did. To solve it, you couldn't simply slide another piece in. Instead you had to think differently about how each piece worked. What was once pointed in is now pointed out. What was once on the top is now on the bottom.

To leverage behavioral science to its greatest ends for your goals, you'll have to challenge the long-held conventions about how healthcare companies and advocates engage people. Advocating for that kind of new approach isn't easy. It requires deep insight and bold moves that interrupt some thinking that healthcare is pretty comfortable with.

A story about sports as seen through the eyes a couple of financial strategists, Cliff Asness and Aaron Brown, seems really relevant here.[2,3]

Asness and Brown believe that, across the entire sport of hockey, coaches are doing something suboptimally. They're pulling the goalie at the wrong time. You know how this play goes: if it's late in the game and your team is down by one goal, the coach typically benches the goalie and subs in an extra attacker. It's a tradeoff. The extra attacker increases your team's chances of scoring, but the unguarded goal increases your opponent's chances of scoring, too.

A bold strategy. A bold strategy that according to Asness and Brown is executed at entirely the wrong time.

Coaches pull goalies in the final minutes because it's part of hockey tradition. It's the way they know. But what if they looked at the data? That's what our two economic strategists did. They played moneyball with pucks.

They built a computer model that showed the most effective time to pull the goalie. If the team is down by one goal, then pull the goalie when there are 5 minutes and 40 seconds left. Down by two goals? It's even sooner: 11 minutes and 40 seconds.

Imagine that. That's the kind of insight healthcare and life science leaders are looking for today. **What would we do differently if we could see healthcare interactions clearly instead of through the lens of the conventions and traditions of our category? How could we change our organizations if we were able to act on what people really need, as opposed to what we've done before? How can we leverage behavioral science to deliver our own game-changing strategy?**

In This Book

To build that comprehensive picture of what we know about behavioral science and make it actionable for your work or your business, we've divided this book into two parts:

Part 1: The Nine Principles of Influence

We aren't so different.

When you think about how people are fundamentally wired, we have a lot in common. We all have basic needs and are uncomfortable when they're interrupted. We are all defined in part by the social connections in our lives. We all behave irrationally at moments – and probably wouldn't have it any other way.

Those are just some of the core behavioral principles that make us human. You will see how these principles can act as barriers that wire us to resist health behavior change as well as how they have the power to activate change.

In Part 1, we'll unpack 9 Principles of Influence; each is founded on a core understanding of behavioral science. These principles both help explain the *why* behind the perplexing problems facing the healthcare industry and provide actionable strategies for innovating communications, products or services.

Part 2: The (Behavioral) Science of Segmenting

We can be really different.

Part two is a much smaller part of the book. In fact, you might simply call it a tenth chapter. But, it's critical in showing how we move from these broad principles to customizing behavioral design for specific segments of your audience.

In this section you'll dig into three specific ways to segment your audience to get even closer to what specifically motivates them. Understanding these segments will change the interventions you create, leading to simple personalization schemas that keep your audience engaged and motivated as they move from awareness into interest, interest into commitment, commitment into action, and action into resilience.

Healthy Nudges How To

Use this book as your guidebook and action plan. You'll find worksheets and thought starters along the way. It's time to literally put pen to paper on the possibilities of behavioral science in healthcare communications.

BOOK PLANNING GUIDE

What do you most want to know about behavioral science and how to better engage and motivate healthcare stakeholders? Note your early questions and ideas here to focus your time.

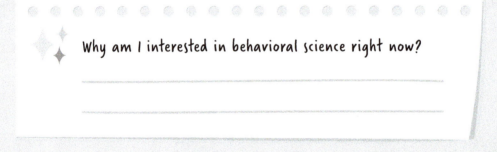

Why am I interested in behavioral science right now?

What decisions might be informed by what I read and learn?

Who am I most likely going to want to talk to about these principles?

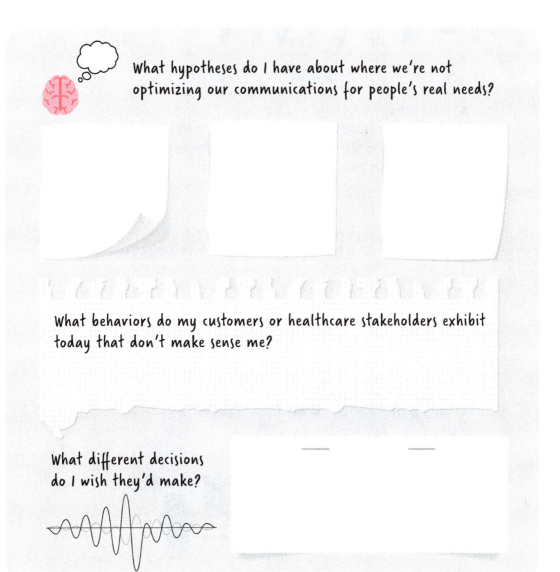

What hypotheses do I have about where we're not optimizing our communications for people's real needs?

What behaviors do my customers or healthcare stakeholders exhibit today that don't make sense me?

What different decisions do I wish they'd make?

For most readers, we believe this book will do two things: help you understand your customers or stakeholders better and give you the language and frameworks to talk about what drives people to change. Many of these concepts are understandings you likely already feel at a gut level. The principles will bring them to life in ways that are focused, actionable, and ready to introduce to your full team. Let's get started.

WHAT IS MOTIVATION?

It's a Guy Riding an Elephant.[4]

Motivation is the drive behind our behavior. It's the reason people act the way they do. Lack of motivation is the gap between what we say and what we do. Or, said a better way: it's the gap between our intentions and our actions.

For example, the vast majority of people say that clinical trials for cancer medications are a good thing and even personally express the intention to enroll in one if they were facing cancer. But fewer than 1:20 people fighting cancer actually do.[5]

1:20

Or, when patients accept a new treatment plan from a doctor, 1:3 never even fill the first prescription.[6]

1:3

What about the healthcare intentions we're entirely in control of?

ONE CLUE: January **12** is the date most people abandon their new year's resolutions.

The science says that all these healthcare realities (we can't even properly call them choices) are driven by two kinds of processing: automatic and reflective. In *Thinking, Fast and Slow,* renowned psychologist and winner of the Nobel Prize in Economics **Daniel Kahneman** described those two modes this way:[7]

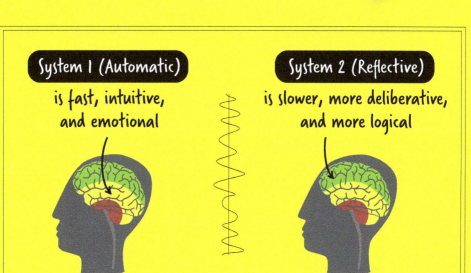

System 1 (Automatic) is fast, intuitive, and emotional

System 2 (Reflective) is slower, more deliberative, and more logical

The challenge for healthcare: automatic behaviors are like the elephant, and those important reflective ones are just the rider. But the elephant certainly holds a lot of sway.

This book helps readers look at healthcare change through both lenses – the automatic behaviors that are outside of our conscious thought and the reflective ones that give that rider a lot more control.

Part 1: The Nine Principles of Influence

The best experiences in the consumer world today are frictionless. It's almost easier to continue the journey to sign-up or purchase than it is to step off the path. Click on a compelling Instagram® promotion, sign up with one click, confirm your information, get congratulated on success, and then just wait a quick 24 hours for the good stuff to arrive.

The healthcare world is anything but frictionless. The complexity can seem nearly endless: from competing stakeholder priorities to conflicting information to constraints on choice.

But friction doesn't just come from logistics or systemic limitations; it comes from context. From the ways we talk to people and the nuance with which we do – or more often do not – understand what motivates them.

We've identified nine principles of behavior that can help healthcare organizations and advocates reduce friction and promote change. These evidence-based insights can be leveraged to design new interventions and communications that will drive change.

The Nine Principles of Influence

Principle 1: Core psychological needs drive us

Principle 2: Mental processing is limited

Principle 3: Irrational shortcuts guide decision making

Principle 4: We understand the present through the past

Principle 5: Self is a social phenomenon

Principle 6: Goals organize our behavior

Principle 7: Context is critical to our habits

Principle 8: We constantly redefine normal

Principle 9: Motivation is fleeting

For each principle, we'll reveal:

What it means about people

Why it wires us to resist change

How to use it to activate change

Although each of these principles is presented separately in an effort to simplify the underlying science, none of them operates in isolation. These principles are what make us uniquely human. At any one moment, they interact in different ways to influence behaviors.

PRINCIPLE I:

 Core Psychological Needs Drive Us

THE COMMUNICATOR'S ESSENTIALS:

Underlying needs

We have core psychological needs that are as real and powerful as basic physical needs.

Conflict and Distress

Many healthcare situations and decisions can violate those needs, creating stress and conflict that suddenly come to the forefront.

Poor Decisions

That conflict can sometimes lead us to act in counterintuitive ways that may be against our best interests and limit our ability to change.

Reduce Stress

Communications and programs need to mitigate the negative impact of healthcare change on core needs.

Amplify Motivation

Fulfilling core needs as part of behavioral design can amplify the impact of a communication and move people from "I have to" to "I want to."

Principle 1: Core Psychological Needs Drive Us

Walk into your average corporate office in July, and you'll both feel that sub-zero air conditioner blaring and quickly remember one of your core biologic needs: warmth. Time to pull on the sweater.

Intrinsic human needs go far beyond the physical (like food, shelter and water). They extend to the emotional and social drivers of our wants and desires. These six are particularly relevant to healthcare experiences:

	Core Need	How It Can Be Violated
Autonomy	The need to feel independent, be in control and trust that our beliefs are valued	Being pressured by others Feeling that we are being given no choice Facing uncontrollable life events
Mastery	The need to feel competent and able to manage the world and challenges we face	Overwhelming new situations Negative feedback on our performance Not being given the opportunity to try something new for ourselves
Belonging	The need to feel connected to others, to feel understood and cared for	Being seen as an outsider Experiencing interpersonal conflict Feeling separated from others
Security	The need to feel emotionally and physically safe from anticipated harm	Not knowing what to expect Not understanding why something is happening Having scarce tangible resources (e.g. money)
Purpose	The need to feel that we are accomplishing things of value to the world beyond ourselves	Having opportunities cut short Feeling that time is being wasted Being put on a "treadmill" with no signal of progress
Fairness	The need to feel that we are being treated the same as others, are getting our due, and are not being prejudged	Witnessing others being discriminated against Being subject to arbitrary rules and procedures Having the fruits of our labor seem small in proportion to our investment

Just like the need for food or water, these needs operate in the background, at a subconscious level, until the moment they don't. When the ability to fulfill these needs is threatened, they immediately move to the forefront and may change our behavior.

Unfulfilled needs might leave us feeling anything from a subtle pang of emotional discomfort to full-blown anxiety. **Those unfulfilled needs are a force that can rapidly bring us to do counterintuitive things. A force that can override our rational decision making, letting bad feelings lead to bad decisions.**

How core psychological needs can wire us to resist change

 IN SHORT: *We sometimes resist change when one of our core needs is violated.*

When people's core needs are threatened, they can feel stressed, frustrated, and riddled with doubt, pain or fear. Any one of those negative emotions can lead someone to instinctively move away from adversity, causing them to lose focus, react reflexively rather than deliberately, or retreat into old habits.

There may be no better example than the diagnosis itself. A diagnosis violates the fundamental need for security. Because treatment may require us to do certain things at certain times that place new restrictions on our lives, the treatment can erode our sense of autonomy. Living with the disease can leave us feeling alienated, pulled away from our connection or association with others.

The result: unbelievable friction. The response to that friction might look like something as big as refusal of care, but it can also come in the form of subtler resistance.

Information Lockout

One example of how resistance presents itself is information avoidance: preventing or delaying access to available but potentially unwanted information.

We might wait out a troubling symptom long after we know we should have talked to a doctor, avoid reading about a treatment plan or diagnosis, or keep important information from a loved one who could help us.

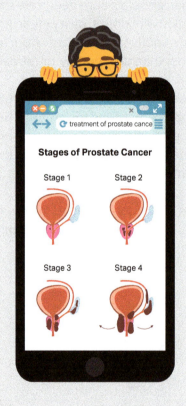

That behavior doesn't just manifest in patients. It's how care partners cope with having their core needs violated, too. One study found that over half of participants would not want to know if their spouse had a genetic vulnerability.[8]

Another study of the spouses of men fighting prostate cancer found that one of their key coping mechanisms was to avoid learning more about the disease.[9]

In this context, resistance is actually the easiest path. Overcoming avoidance, learning to cope with difficult situations, and making the necessary changes?

That's the real work.

Although the larger healthcare system is founded on good intent, there are important violations that can leave emotional and social needs unfulfilled for both patients and their physicians.

Need Violation: Mastery

The days or weeks immediately following a diagnosis are rife with moments that steal our sense of control: from making decisions with no experience to trying to make sense of medical jargon to needing (or wanting) to ask the doctor the same questions over and over again just to have a basic sense of what is going on.

Need Violation: Belonging

If a treatment stands in the way of social connections, it can violate the need for belonging. For example, a person living with diabetes might be told to lower their A1C measurement to best manage the underlying disease. What if achieving that goal requires dietary changes that conflict with existing rituals around food, family and community that are the true expressions of social connectivity for that patient?

Need Violation: Fairness

The inability to understand an insurance or reimbursement plan may ignite a feeling of unfairness, especially when the calculations are not transparent and the results seem different than expectations set by the insurer, doctor or friends.

Need Violation: Purpose

Physicians are working in a space that requires them to be both clinically competent and truly empathetic with their patients.[10] In practice, being both is almost impossible, driving many to ignore their feelings and focus on the practicalities of medicine. This may not be particularly satisfying, aligned with the reason they pursued medicine, or good for their wellbeing. Ultimately, it can **lead to burnout and other challenges.**[11]

The Burnout Multiplier Effect

What happens when doctors' core needs are violated and they are left feeling burnout?

A recent study found that, among those that expressed feelings of depression, the following statistics emerge about how it impacts their relationships with patients and peers:[12]

35% said
"I am easily exasperated with patients."

26% said
"I'm less motivated to be careful about taking patient notes."

47% said
"I'm more easily exasperated with staff and peers."

16% said
"I express my frustration in front of patients."

Self-report findings have also indicated that burnout is associated with an increased risk of patient safety incidents, poorer quality of care and reduced patient satisfaction.[13]

2x

the risk of portraying low professionalism

the odds of involvement in patient safety incidents

increase in patient-reported low satisfaction

Certainly, some difficult healthcare situations, if they're not too overwhelming, may propel people to take action in response to threats to their needs. What's more, over time, even the most challenging experiences can be reframed as meeting core needs. Someone who successfully fought cancer or is living well with HIV might talk about what they've learned from the experience or how it's made them stronger. Whatever the path, the key is the desire to fulfill core needs like mastery, purpose and belonging.

How core psychological needs can be used to activate change

 IN SHORT: *We're more open to change when it fulfills one of our core needs.*

To increase motivation, interventions or communications need to do two things:

Recognize and mitigate violations of core needs + Amplify the power of those core needs

The natural way to use this behavioral principle to design change is bolstering the ability of people to fulfill their core needs. **The clearest way to do that is to change the context from "I have to" to "I want to."** Interventions and communications can do that through approaches that help people:

Set their own goals rather than having goals assigned

Learn about a subject at their own pace and come back with questions later

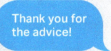

Connect with people in similar situations

Balance the needs of the family with the needs of the patient

Become a mentor or role model for someone else

Preview what their upcoming experience might be like

Acknowledge and take time to deal with the emotional impact of the situation

Regain a sense of normalcy

Incorporate something fun or enjoyable into their list of "have tos"

The other critical component of activating change is ensuring that we've mitigated threats to core needs. If, for example, a cost conversation will absolutely violate a sense of fairness, can we intentionally design communications and tools to increase transparency and deepen understanding about the *why*?

Try this **worksheet** to design interventions around core needs: ⟶

Core Needs Worksheet

WHO are we designing a behavioral intervention for:

Healthcare Professional

Patient

What point are they at in the healthcare journey:

Having an unexplained symptom

Getting a diagnosis

Preparing for a medical procedure

Adjusting lifestyle to take care of medical condition

Other

What do they have to do to be successful: *(e.g. make complex treatment decisions; change eating behavior)*	⊛
What decision do you want to effect: *(e.g. talk to your doctor about a troubling symptom)*	✓ ✗

What core needs might be violated?	**How?** *(Describe the approach)*	Can we mitigate the violation?
☐ Autonomy		
☐ Mastery		
☐ Belonging		
☐ Security		
☐ Purpose		
☐ Fairness		

What core need might you amplify to help activate/embrace change?

What core needs might be violated?	**How?** *(Describe the approach)*	What specific intervention or communication would help?
☐ Autonomy		
☐ Mastery		
☐ Belonging		
☐ Security		
☐ Purpose		
☐ Fairness		

PRINCIPLE 2:

 Mental Processing Is Limited

THE COMMUNICATOR'S ESSENTIALS:

Attention Is Limited

Limitations on what we can process or think about at any one time can impact how deeply we process critical health decisions and how well we can manage change.

Decision Weight

From the number of options available to the stress naturally embedded in healthcare discussions, decisions can frequently feel overwhelming.

Growing Complexity

The multiplier of this very human challenge is that people are being asked to make more complex decisions than ever before.

Curated Choices

The antidote to overchoice starts with simplifying the options to reduce friction and overload, potentially reducing the options down to just one: the default.

Voice of Choice

It's important that those choices come from a trusted voice, an architect of selections that the customer will know are in her best interest.

Principle 2: Mental Processing Is Limited

How many things can you remember at a time? If you're like most people, the number you can hold in your working memory – without memorization tricks – is about three or four.[14] Compare that to the amount of information thrown at a physician on an average day or at a patient in a critical moment.

For behavioral design, this isn't an issue of changing what we are mentally capable of but how a healthcare communication or intervention can best engage those limited resources to break through and make critical connections in the moments they're needed most.

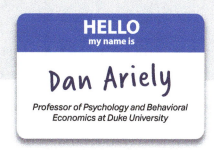

"We build products that work with our physical limitations. Chairs, shoes, and cars are all designed to complement and enhance our physical capabilities. If we take some of the same lessons we've learned from working with our physical limitations and apply them to things that are affected by our cognitive limitations—insurance policies, retirement plans, and healthcare—we'll be able to design more effective policies and tools that are more useful in the world."

HELLO
my name is

Dan Ariely

Professor of Psychology and Behavioral Economics at Duke University

How limited mental processing can wire us to resist change

 IN SHORT: *With limited mental processing power, complex choices can be overwhelming.*

Big changes are taking place in healthcare that require people to make more complex decisions – about care, cost, and consequences – than ever before. Yet each of those new choices challenges what people can consciously process at any one time, creating gaps in how deeply information is processed and how effectively it will promote change.

0004 Department of the Brain
Simplified **Individual Tax**   *Four conditions are fundamentally most taxing to the brain:*

☐ **Complex information**	☐ **Number of options**
☐ **Uncertain outcomes**	☐ **Stressful situations**

Complexity of information: On its face, it would seem like more thorough information is better, but when information gets complex, people tend to limit their focus to the most familiar concepts or take mental shortcuts, as you'll read about in the next principle.

Simplify With A Mnemonic

Short, memorable principles are a time-proven way to cut through the clutter of complexity and deliver actionable content people can remember and quickly pull from memory.

Alone. Back. Crib.

From Tamiflu's Flu F.A.C.T.S. (fever, aches, chills, tiredness, sudden onset) to public health's A.B.C.s (alone, back, crib) of sleep to prevent Sudden Unexplained Infant Deaths, these simple mnemonics make new behaviors easy to learn. In fact, the new behaviors become something you don't even have to think about.

By the way: bonus if you can make them rhyme.

Number of options: The amount of choice in healthcare today – from the options in any one category to the potential to customize any of them to your needs – is overwhelming. In fact, studies have shown that the presence of too many choices quickly becomes demotivating.[15] More than demotivating, an overload of options may end up paralyzing people into making no decision or pushing them into decisions that are against their own best interest.

Uncertain outcomes: Have you read Blaise Pascal's study of decisions known as the Theory of Expected Value?[16] It says that when faced with two uncertain options, all a person has to do is determine the positive or negative values of the possible outcomes associated with one option, multiply them by their probabilities of occurrence, sum the results, then do it all over again for the alternative, and voilà, the alternative with the high score wins. Easy, right? Not when you're dealing with a challenge in a field you know very little about that has unbelievably personal stakes. Uncertain outcomes can quickly lead people to resist decisions and resist change.

How Language Changes Decisions

Because mental resources are limited, how the situation is framed up can have a strong impact on the decisions we make

Much of the modern history of behavioral economics was written by two psychologists named Daniel Kahneman and Amos Tversky. Their seminal work helped reverse the long-held assumption that human decision making is fundamentally rational.

In one experiment, they demonstrated that phrasing the exact same problem in terms of gaining as opposed to losing would significantly—maybe even radically—change people's decisions.[17] The duo gave a group two scenarios of hypothetical medical treatment options for a deadly disease.

~~~~~~~~~~~~~~~~~~~~ Scenario 1: ~~~~~~~~~~~~~~~~~~~~

If a certain treatment is given to 600 people with the disease,

  200 lives will be saved.

If a riskier treatment is given, there is a $\frac{1}{3}$ chance that **all will be saved** and a $\frac{2}{3}$ chance of **saving no one.**

~~~~~~~~~~~~~~~~~~~~ Scenario 2: ~~~~~~~~~~~~~~~~~~~~

If a certain treatment is given to 600 people with the disease,

400 people will definitely die.

If a riskier treatment is given, there is a $\frac{1}{3}$ chance that **no one will die** and a $\frac{2}{3}$ chance that **all 600 people will die.**

Notice that Scenario 2 was framed as lives lost rather than lives gained.

Although, if you do the math, the expected outcomes across all of these choice options are exactly the same, the majority of the group that was shown Scenario 1 chose saving 200 people for sure, even though that meant 400 people would definitely not be saved. And the people who were shown Scenario 2? They decided to gamble, risking the lives of those same 200 people if they thought they could avoid all 600 dying.

~~~~~~~~~~ What was different? Absolutely nothing—
except the way the problem was described. ~~~~~~~~~~

Stressful situations: Dealing with acutely stressful events may require lots of effort and can deplete attentional resources, which can have a big impact on decision making. In fact, a recent study found that risk aversion and antisocial behavior increase as early as an hour after a stress event.[18] Beyond those initial findings, the authors also noted that stressed individuals tend to fixate on themselves rather than consider the negative impact on others, an interesting dimension in the socially-interconnected world of life and health.

Mental Processing of Jam Choices (Yes, Jam)

One of the most intriguing studies demonstrating how choice is at once appealing and debilitating was conducted by Sheena Iyengar, a professor of business at Columbia University and the author of *The Art of Choosing*.[19]

The study took place in a gourmet market where Iyengar set up a sampling station for Wilkin & Sons jams. The station was reset every few hours – sometimes with a selection of 24 jams, sometimes just 6. Regardless of the selection, customers tasted, on average, two jams. Each received a coupon for $1 off their purchase.

~~~~ Which jam selection drew the largest crowds? ~~~~

60% of samplers stopped by the larger assortment

40% of samplers stopped by the smaller assortment

But, only **3 percent** of the visitors to the large assortment bought a jar of jam compared to **30 percent** who tasted from the smaller collection.

Take away: people typically say they want lots of choice, but that doesn't mean it will help them make decisions.

How limited mental processing can be managed to allow for change

 IN SHORT: *Focus choices and deliver them through a trusted voice.*

All of this information, these moments of overchoice, are coming to healthcare stakeholders at a moment of declining consumer trust in key institutions, from insurance companies to life science innovators and hospitals.

As we look at key strategies to activate change by leveraging the principle that mental processing is limited, we'll consider two equally important levers:

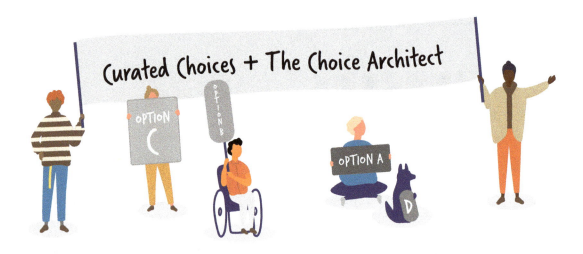

Because mental resources are limited, it's less taxing and often more pleasing for people to select from among a much smaller number of choices—even down to one.

Defaults: Defaults set up a path of least resistance. When you think about behavioral design, defaults are a favorite in the choice architecture toolbox. From organ donation to retirement planning, strategic default choices have been a powerful way to help people effortlessly accept an option.

Organ donation options tend to be very similar across countries and geographies. They either ask participants to opt in (check here if you want to be an organ donor) or opt out (check here if you do not want to be an organ donor). The difference in sign up rates between the two can be dramatic: in the high nineties in countries that have opt-out organ donation and in the tens for countries that ask for the opt in.[20] Employee retirement plans work a similar way: one study found that employees were 50 percent more likely to participate when they were automatically enrolled upon starting employment.[21]

Defaults have effectively been used to guide more complex decision making in healthcare as well. In one study, to increase the number of appropriate patients in cardiac rehab following a heart attack, the electronic health record platform was programmed to identify eligible patients and make a default referral. Physicians' task was simplified to signing orders in a template or opting out of the recommending referral.[22]

Limited choices: A more focused set of choices can be equally effective, especially if the selection is focused on what a peer group or similarly-profiled healthcare user might choose. Help people navigate information more effectively by showing them the funnel of choices that led to the few they truly need to select from.

Curating Choice At Lunch

Google's company cafeteria is quite popular for many reasons. It's open 24/7, there's a great variety of food, and it doesn't hurt that everything's free. But it's also designed to promote health and environmental values (local, organic, sustainable).[23]

MENU

Proteins

Veggies

Carbs

Google uses strategies to direct employees to healthier choices: putting the healthiest products at eye level, using smaller plates for portion control, and making vegetables predominant on its shelves. The only places on the campus where employees pay for food are vending machines, and there, items with healthier nutritional content are cheaper than less healthy options.

Its food labeling also helps make healthy choices easy by flagging all food with traffic lights: green (eat anytime), yellow (once in a while), or red (not often, please). It bases the decisions about which food goes where on the Harvard School of Public Health's healthy eating pyramid. It labels foods at the top of the Harvard pyramid red, the ones in the middle yellow, and those at the bottom green.

But who sets up these choices?

A critical player in helping navigate the principle of limited mental resources is the choice architect: a sponsor or person behind the scenes dictating what choices are available and how the limited choice is being teed up for the decision maker. In an era of waning trust, that source's credibility is critical. People need to believe that the architect's intentions align with their own.[24]

Ethics Check

Behavioral science is sometimes referred as "the dark arts" because of concerns that it can be used to manipulate behavior. For those thinking about incorporating nudges to engage stakeholders, asking these basic questions can help surface possible ethical concerns:[25,26]

- Is there adequate transparency as to the intent of the intervention?

- Does the intervention respect stakeholders' independence and autonomy?

- Are there any unintended consequences that should be avoided?

- Does the intervention put any other group at a disadvantage?

We believe staying focused on helping stakeholders make well-informed decisions and follow through on the decisions they've deemed best for themselves is both highly ethical and critical to helping people realize the health intentions they've set for themselves.

Try this **worksheet** to determine how your stakeholder's mental energy is being sapped and uncover ways you can make considering a change easier. ⟶

Mental Load Worksheet

WHO
are we designing a
behavioral intervention for:

Healthcare Professional

Patient

Decision moment that person is at:

HIGH
IMPACT

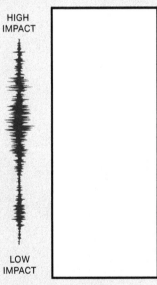

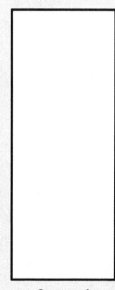

LOW
IMPACT

Complexity of
Information

Number of
Options

Uncertainty of
Outcomes

Stress of
Situation

What are 1-3 ways you could simplify the mental load?

1

2

3

PRINCIPLE 3:

 Irrational Shortcuts Guide Decision Making

THE COMMUNICATOR'S ESSENTIALS:

Needed Shortcuts

We all have shorthand and shortcuts that we use to simplify decision making, even if they make those decisions somewhat irrational.

Cognitive Biases

These systemic shortcuts are core to the human condition; they fill our gaps in knowledge to fuel quick choices.

Mental Models

This category of shortcuts varies by person or audience type and is shaped by their past experience and views of the world.

Less Than Perfect Necessity

We are always finding new ways to lighten the thinking burden, which means that we may, at times, make faulty on-the-fly choices.

New Nudges

Those same biases fuel powerful natural levers that can promote behavior change.

Principle 3: Irrational Shortcuts Guide Decision Making

You've probably recovered from the puzzle in the introduction by now; so, how about another game? An American teenage classic: *Would You Rather*?

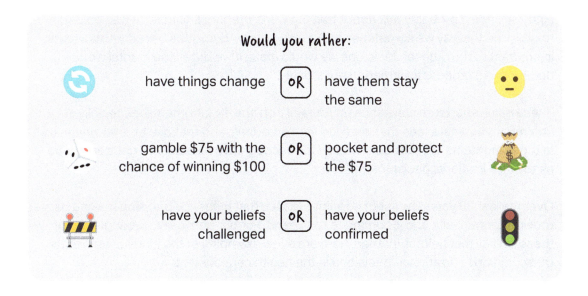

On one hand, it's a silly game, but on the other, you probably had instant answers to every question. You were able to preserve your mental energy and not think too hard because there are certain shortcuts we all use to simplify new decisions.

Cognitive biases or systemic tendencies (such as the tendency to avoid loss) have been shown to influence some of the decisions people make. They are core to the human condition, and they're largely what will be covered here.

As you get deeper into behavioral science you may also come across the term "mental model." Mental models are shaped by people's interactions with the world around them, such as experience of a disease. What's important to remember is that mental models can be audience specific and can impact how people think about a choice, a conversation or even a company.

How irrational shortcuts can wire us to resist change

 *IN SHORT:* *Our built-in biases operate under the radar, making it difficult to correct for them.*

First, we should probably talk about that big word: irrational. That term was coined to describe the way we sometimes make less optimal decisions based on shortcuts in contrast to the rational decisions we would make if we did all the mental work necessary to process information objectively.

These quick shortcuts can set us up for faulty on-the-fly judgments, especially in unfamiliar circumstances that are filled with emotions, and that can be overwhelming. In those moments, it's particularly easy for our cognitive biases to fill gaps and drive us to make irrational decisions.

Over the last 20 years the list of cognitive biases that influence decision making has grown exponentially, and it continues to expand. For our purposes, cataloging all of these isn't all that helpful. Instead, here are a few examples of the kinds of shortcuts that could drive "irrational" decisions in the health care context:

Optimism Bias: When we look into the future, we tend to overestimate the likelihood of positive outcomes and underestimate that of negative events. We might discount the potential of receiving a chronic diagnosis, losing a spouse or job, or being robbed, while overestimating how likely we are to make more money in the future, live to an old age, or see our kids win a coveted spot on the team. Basically, we tend to think we have better odds than others.

Status Quo Bias: The present is a powerful reference point and we have a strong preference for the current state of affairs. Anything different from that baseline can feel disruptive and even like a loss. That status quo bias can lead us to resist change and try to keep things just the way they are.

Loss Aversion: How did you respond to that question earlier about making the $75 bet? The loss aversion bias is the tendency to be more affected by losses than we are by equivalent gains. Our fears are amplified when we think a decision might result in a loss or that we will lose something if we make a change.

Confirmation Bias: This is one precept of behavioral science that has definitely reached the mainstream. Confirmation bias is the very human tendency to seek out information, and interpret it in such a way, that confirms what we already believe. It leads us to stop looking for new information or exploring alternatives that conflict with our original beliefs and assumptions.

Self-Serving Bias: We have the tendency to perceive ourselves in an overly favorable manner (these authors certainly know we do). The self-serving bias may lead us to discount how much our day-to-day behavior really matters when things aren't going our way, leading us to avoid taking responsibility for our actions and seeing which changes we need to make. When things go awry, we tend to blame external forces; when things go right, that's all us.

Availability Bias: We tend to overweight information that readily comes to mind. Situations that are weird, unusual, or very dramatic are sticky that way. They quickly pop to mind. They fool us into overgeneralizing what we remember about those situations to all situations. For example, for physicians, the hardest patient case they've dealt with may quickly stand out, leading them to look for those same characteristics in the next case.

In addition to these biases, we also have our own personal rules of thumb— comfortable ways of doing things we've learned that can put us on autopilot. For example, physicians may have rules of thumb that help prioritize spending time with the patients they perceive to be most in need. However, that may prevent them from looking at other important information. For example, when working with a patient with a deep understanding of diabetes, a physician may not inquire about adherence or double check that she is rotating injection sites.[27]

All of these small shortcuts wire us to make quick judgments, when it might be better to make more thoughtful ones. They make it easy to effectively resist change in ways that feel incredibly intuitive in a given moment.

Not every bias needs to be taken into account for every behavioral design project. We pick and choose the most important intervention points based on the situation and the audience. For example, when asking healthcare professionals to try something that is new or uncomfortable, Loss Aversion Bias could play a big role. When educating consumers about a population risk (e.g. risk of getting the flu), Optimism Bias could be important to demonstrating the real risk faced by each person.

Wait, Isn't This The Era of the Empowered Consumer?

Headlines around the world have declared the Age of Consumerism in healthcare, a time when every individual is empowered with the data, reviews and price transparency needed to make an informed decision on every aspect of health.

Behavioral science sees the reality of healthcare very differently.
First, consumer behavior isn't the powerful proxy for healthcare or medical decision making we might like it to be. One fundamental reason: these shoppers don't want to be healthcare customers. People don't choose to be sick; they buy things like medicines strictly out of necessity.

Second, behavioral economics has clearly demonstrated that we aren't necessarily methodical or purely rational consumers. Yet, it remains easy for companies to assume that people will be when it comes to the cost/benefit decisions related to healthcare, even though these decisions are more unfamiliar, complicated, and emotionally charged than the ones we make standing in an aisle at a big box store.

It's not realistic to expect that the impact of efforts to fully empower healthcare consumers will scale the same way we've seen other consumer change happen.

How irrational shortcuts can activate change

 IN SHORT: *Even the strongest biases can be flipped to healthy nudges.*

For all the challenges they present, shortcuts set the stage for some of the most natural behavioral nudges. When designing a new communication or intervention, think about leveraging those natural biases in ways that help people reach their overall health goals. The right nudge can either reinforce comprehension of information or make it easier to implement decisions that feel like they've already been made.

Let's return to some of our biases from above and see how they could be flipped to have a positive impact on the healthcare stakeholder. For example:

Bias	Hold back change	Activate change
Status Quo Bias	Feeling that anything different from the status quo will be a lot of work.	Programs that reduce burden or have set-it-and-forget-it features (such as pre-scheduled medical follow ups, automatic enrollments, or programmed medication refills) may trigger our preference to stay the course.
Confirmation bias	Tendency to seek out information, and/or interpret it in such a way, that confirms what we already believe.	Program benefits that connect to things we already believe in can be easier to adopt.
Loss Aversion	Amplification of fears when we think that a decision might result in a loss or that we will lose something if we make a change.	Interventions that create a sense of anticipated regret – that something will be worse in the future if you don't follow through on a new behavior – can help people make decisions through the lens of protecting their future self. This type of nudge strategy has been effective in changing behavior in categories as diverse as condom use, exercise and cancer screening.[28-30] User note: these nudges work most effectively when they're subtle (and don't feel like emotional blackmail).
Availability Bias	Tendency to overly weight information that we can easily recall.	Interventions that use repeated exposure and/or well-timed interactions can help keep the most relevant information top of mind at decision points that matter.

While these nudges will sometimes be effective, at other times, we truly have to block the shortcuts to help a person think deeply about a choice and ultimately make the best, most informed decision.

Often, that can be done by creating intentional opportunities to challenge our own assumptions in safe environments.

For example, Genentech created an opportunity for doctors to evaluate their own behavior in a private moment of self-reflection.[31] The program started with a crystalized insight: 50–60 percent of people diagnosed with lung cancer aren't smokers. Yet they're left feeling like it's their fault. Very few are told to fight. They're told to go home and be with their families. They're left feeling like it's their fault.

Doctors subconsciously look for evidence (via confirmation bias) that something in the patient's behavior, most often smoking, contributed to the disease.

That's why Genentech funded the Lung Cancer Project; they believed the stigmas around lung cancer were impeding care. The brand partnered with a group out of Harvard called Project Implicit that measures feelings outside of your conscious thinking. Their study uncovered hidden misperceptions about lung cancer from caregivers, patients, healthcare providers and the general public. The findings were presented at ASCO, and a coalition of Genentech and 20 advocacy and industry organizations continue to share the research to remove the stigma and other barriers to each person getting the care they need and deserve.

Although the advocacy work has since expanded to websites, social channels, and powerful interventions, it started with a self-assessment, giving every doctor the opportunity to compare their personal bias to that of peers.

In another example, from the Netherlands, a program to provide healthcare professionals with another perspective on mammogram results got peers involved by having two experts review every mammogram. When physicians disagreed, a specific process helped them adjudicate the final result. The false positive rate is now half that of what it is in the United States.[32]

Try this **worksheet** to design interventions around mental shortcuts: $\longrightarrow$

Mental Shortcuts Worksheet

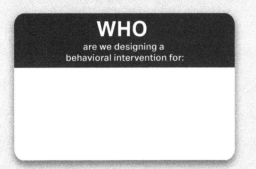

WHO are we designing a behavioral intervention for:

Healthcare Professional

Patient

 What healthcare behavior are you trying to change?

 What mental shortcuts do you think are most likely to be impacting this moment of potential change?

Bias	How could it hold back change?	How could it be used to activate change?
☐ Optimism Bias ✹		
☐ Status Quo Bias		
☐ Loss Aversion		
☐ Confirmation Bias ✓		
☐ Self-Serving Bias		
☐ Availability Bias		
☐ _____ Bias		

Existing "Rules of Thumb" likely triggered by the situation:

☐ _____
☐ _____

How could you interrupt the bias and give people a chance to think deeply:

Bias

PRINCIPLE 4:

 We Understand The Present Through The Past

THE COMMUNICATOR'S ESSENTIALS:

Gut Choices

We navigate unfamiliar situations by leveraging experiences we've had before to make quick assessments about the present.

Important Inferences

Those assessments aren't objective; they're inferences and judgment calls, often about important things like what will be good or bad, scary or safe.

The Limiting Lens

That personal "meaning machine" can limit our ability to take in new information by leading us to see only what we want to see.

Start With Experience

The biggest missed question in all of healthcare is: what previous experience do you have? (With this system, this disease, this treatment.)

Open the Aperture

To give people a wider view of the choices or evidence, it's important to reframe, redirect and recode the information.

Principle 4: We Understand The Present Through The Past

Let's say you or a loved one are facing a serious health crisis. You want to fight with everything you can.

The physician offers you three treatment options:
a pill, an injection, and an infusion.

1   2   3

Which one do you choose?

Many people might choose the infusion. Why? Because in a lay person's rough understanding of the most powerful drugs of the last decades, the IV wins. If a drug has to be administered in a clinic, it must be much more powerful than what someone might take at home. It sounds like serious medicine, the big guns.

There are so many situations in which we need to quickly make sense of the world. We walk into an unfamiliar room and just get a feeling. We hear a series of options and pick whichever one feels right on a gut level. Those quick assessments are actually ways we use the past to create meaning about the present. We use a pre-conceived understanding based on the clues or experience we've collected before; we use it to predict what will happen next.

Those assessments aren't just academic—they're filled with implications for things we care about. Is something going to be positive or negative, good or bad, strong or weak? Will it lead to danger or safety, hope or despair?

There are few aspects of our lives that are more rife with unfamiliarity than healthcare. Yet, as communicators or practitioners, we rarely start with the most important question: what's your past experience been?

That experience will have an outsized impact on how a person understands a diagnosis, classifies treatment options, and considers what they'll do next. **Effective healthcare communications are not just about the biology or the algorithm of care but also the psychology of it.** What is a person's experience with each step of treatment? What previous experience do they have with health and healthcare? Which family and friend stories walked in the room with them?

Those answers frame the next experience. They tell you who is coming in with a failure mindset. Who has had five successful treatments before and fully expects this one to be successful, too. Who watched a friend or family member go through something similar and struggle with side effects and co-morbidities they're now terrified of.

How a person feels in a given moment has a big impact on how they interpret that history. Emotional stress, particularly, can cause selective interpretation of memory and more negative expectations.

Why fighting ambiguity with history can wire us to resist change

 IN SHORT: *The past can be a limiting lens.*

These meaning machines we create through experience and emotion are critical to helping us quickly assess unfamiliar situations, but they can also limit our ability to take in new information and embrace healthcare change in five really important ways:

1. **Conflate fact and interpretation:** We can be quick to assume our initial assessment is the most accurate, even when it blurs objective facts and subjective inferences. This can limit our ability to read new information or have new conversations with a mind open to what the range of possibilities or data really is.

   A simple example that everyone who has ever fought for control of the thermostat will understand:

    Fact: "It's 87 degrees outside."

   An interpretation draws a conclusion about that fact, for example: "It's unbearably hot outside."

   While that is a perfectly reasonable conclusion if it is 87 degrees outside, it's still a matter of perception and based on individual experiences, likes and dislikes. Someone might interpret 87 degrees to be just right because they've only ever lived in Southern California where the climate is dry; another might interpret it to mean that it's too hot, because they've lived in Mississippi where humid days are common.

2. **Pick unhelpful history:** We can pull meaning forward that doesn't necessarily apply to us, sometimes in ways that undercut motivation to act or diminish our belief that we have the power to change a particular circumstance.

   For example, one study found that people living with heart failure were likely to chalk up their symptoms to old age, based on the experiences of people around them. They blamed age or other co-morbid conditions, like arthritis, for what were truly much more serious and actionable warning signs, like feeling generally weak or being unable to walk to the bathroom.[33]

3. **See what we want to see:** Past clues can narrow our thinking to experiences that have benefited us before. Or, we may interpret another person's behavior based on how others have behaved before.

   According to the Institute for Healthcare Advancement, a common communication error made in patient-physician dialog is when a physician confuses a patient response of "yes" or a head nod with consent to treatment, when in reality it may just be a gesture of politeness.[34]

4. **Make selective interpretations:** In ambiguous situations, without enough evidence, we also use history to create selective views of what applies to "people like me," actively blocking out data points and examples that don't match our understanding of who we are and how we're different.

   One example often used by healthcare-focused behavioral scientists is the smoking athlete. She runs, eats well, considers herself a bit of a health nut. She also smokes. She understands that there are health risks to smoking, but believes they won't impact her as long as she maintains her other healthy habits and smokes less than one pack a day.

   The images she's seen or the experiences she's had with people fighting lung cancer don't look like her; so, she's able to use that selective perception filter to craft an understanding that leaves important medical information behind.

5. **Make incorrect assumptions:** We tend to operate as if our meaning machines are shared by all. In healthcare, this becomes evident when we take a look at cultural differences in the meaning of health, illness, treatments, or role expectations of patient and provider. For example, people from some cultural backgrounds may believe that it is acceptable and even preferred to have bad news kept from the patient.[35] Yet Western doctors are unlikely to ever consider this. They may fully disclose bad news that isn't wanted, causing not only stress but a feeling that an unwritten rule has been violated.

How to use fighting ambiguity with history to activate change

 IN SHORT: *To open the aperture, we have to interrupt the filters.*

Shaking what we think we know is hard to do, but there are some proven strategies for breaking out of existing meaning filters and opening up a wider view of the present:

The 3Rs: reframe, redirect, recode

~~~~~~~~~~~~~~~~~~~ REFRAME ~~~~~~~~~~~~~~~~~~~

Help people reframe an understanding by reinterpreting data or decision-making criteria in a way that's relevant to their particular experience.

One fascinating study about mindset found that reframing could even have a physical impact. A team at Harvard studied how hotel room attendants view and experience exercise. The room attendants described themselves as physically inactive, but their daily work included walking, pushing, lifting – all elements of a great workout. The researchers told one group of the attendants that their work satisfies the Surgeon General's recommendations for an active lifestyle and is, in fact, exercise. The group that received the reframing information both perceived themselves as more active and showed a decrease in weight, blood pressure, body fat, waist-to-hip ratio, and body mass index.[36]

~~~~~~~~~~~~~~~~~~~ REDIRECT ~~~~~~~~~~~~~~~~~~~

Leverage our natural selective attention to draw someone away from their automatic meaning machine with novelty.

For example, in Dubai, women were not proactively seeking breast cancer screening, in large part due to the taboo about talking about it.[37] Yet 44% of the cancers in the Middle East are breast cancers. To break the silence in a sensitive way, Medcare placed a pebble inside the shoes women had taken off to attend prayers or religious education sessions. Upon coming back, the women felt a lump inside their shoes with a note that said simply, "Some Lumps are Not Visible, Breast Check Tips at 1-800-Medcare." 33.3% of recipients called the toll-free number.

RECODE

Use familiar analogs to describe new information to help people easily absorb and remember it. Or piggyback on existing rules of thumb to provide instruction on how to change to make it feel more intuitive. We learn best when we can integrate new knowledge into pre-existing knowledge. If it feels easy, we assume it's true.

For example, in trying to convince a patient to adopt a new daily chronic disease treatment, a helpful analog could simply be that taking that medication on a daily basis is like watering a garden. If you don't start until the plants are wilted and weary, it's far too late.

Or, this example from Brenda Rizzo (VP, Medical Director at GSW Worldwide) trying to convince neurologists to change how they think about treating multiple sclerosis progression: take a sheet of paper and crumple it up, now flatten it back out. See all those scars and wrinkles that remain? OK, do it again. That's what progression is like – each relapse leaves a mark we can never take away.

Try this experience profiles **worksheet** to design interventions that respond to some of the ways we make meaning: ⟶

A New Profile Worksheet

Effective healthcare communications are not just about the biology or the algorithm of care but also the psychology of it.
Let's ask the unexamined question: what has a person's past experience with treatment been like?

Healthcare Professional

Patient

Decision moment that person is at:	

 Imagine (or, better, research!) three different types
of previous experience a patient might have had with treatment

	Profile 1	Profile 2	Profile 3
Previous experience			
What inferences is that patient likely to make based on this experience?			
Do any of those inferences stand in the way of healthcare change?			
Do any of them support healthcare change?			
What specifically could you do with communications or interventions to help this particular patient make the best decision?			

PRINCIPLE 5:

 Self Is A Social Phenomenon

THE COMMUNICATOR'S ESSENTIALS:

Reference Point: People

How we understand and evaluate ourselves is driven both by what we hear from others and by how we believe we compare to them.

Social Norms

Norms benchmark acceptable behavior in a culture or a much smaller peer group; they also tell us what is typical, influencing how we judge our abilities, weaknesses and risks.

Is It Atypical?

We tend to over- or under-estimate what's normal, letting us rationalize or avoid behaviors that could benefit us.

Big Barriers

Social norms can create major barriers to change, because we want to be like the group or don't have a clear role model.

Social Signals

Every norm works two ways. It can limit change. Or it can be the fuel behind change when it signals a new agreement on what's expected and accepted.

Principle 5: Self Is A Social Phenomenon

Do you consider yourself to be healthy? What about: do you exercise enough? How would you rate your diet? Better than most? Worse than most?

Other people are our reference points. Our concepts of ourselves are formed by what we hear directly from others (compliments, criticisms, challenges) as well as what we believe they think about how we compare or what we do.

In order to figure out what others think about us, we are constantly on the watch for clues that help us determine how we are measuring up to others. **We use social norms to judge our abilities, weaknesses, and risks.**

Not Measuring Up Can Have Health Consequences

Stanford researchers dug into the impact of social reference points in a study of physical activity. They wanted to know: does what you believe about your health actually impact your health? And, could how you perceive yourself compared to others actually lead to premature death?

To find out, the team reviewed data on 60,000 U.S. adults from three national data sets. They were most interested in questions that asked individuals if they were more or less active than peers in their age group. The data sets also revealed actual physical activity – giving the Stanford team a view into real vs. perceived levels of exercise.

Then, they compared death records starting some two decades after the first survey. After controlling for actual physical activity, age, illness, and other key health factors, they found that people who believed they were less active than others were 71 percent more likely to have died since their initial survey.[38]

That stark look at comparative belief is just one example of a growing body of research that shows that how we think we compare to others plays an important role in our overall health.

We also look to see what beliefs and behaviors our groups approve of to help us figure out how to fit in or measure ourselves. Those observations and insights influence how we judge others who fall in or out of line with the group's accepted social norms.

Understanding the norms our stakeholders and audiences are responding to lets us understand what's fueling their behavior, which in turn helps us identify forces that directly conflict with the behavior we want to promote.

To uncover various norms, we've developed an approach that examines how three rings of intimacy may be influencing health behavior:

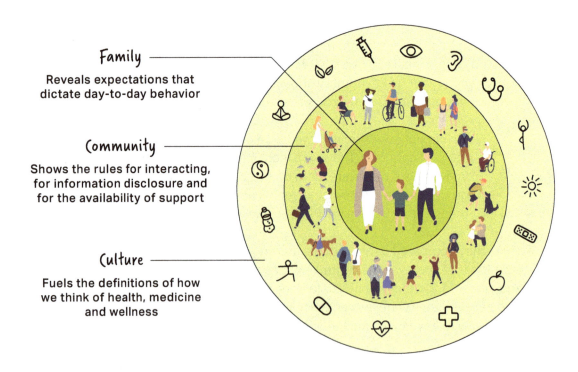

Family
Reveals expectations that dictate day-to-day behavior

Community
Shows the rules for interacting, for information disclosure and for the availability of support

Culture
Fuels the definitions of how we think of health, medicine and wellness

Why "self is a social phenomenon" can wire us to resist change

 IN SHORT: *Information – even great information – can't always get past social norms.*

The people and social groups in our lives impact our thoughts, feelings, and behaviors. In subtle and sometimes not-at-all subtle ways, they change how we interpret ourselves and our worlds. They set standards for what we should expect and what we should accept.

These phenomena can wire us to resist change by causing us to over- or under-estimate what's typical. This can let us rationalize problematic behavior and avoid other behaviors that might have a more beneficial effect in a few significant ways:

Keep it cool	Social norms are powerful barriers to change, especially when changing could make us feel like we have less in common with a highly-regarded group. This lever of resistance has been a significant challenge to changing behavior around habits like seatbelt buckling and smoking.[39-40]
Deprioritize possibilities	Our social roles may be more important to us than reasons to change. Roles like mother, wife, friend, and co-worker are core to our identity. They can cause us to deprioritize new information in order to avoid conflict with what is seen as much more important.
	We may also avoid change to protect a certain self-image.
Never wander alone	We rely on role models to know what to do next. New information can be blocked because it's not coming from one of those credible messengers. That's important because trying something new alone can seem riskier. Lack of social support erodes our confidence and limits the availability of necessary resources (like tangible help). It's linked to higher distress, poorer adherence, and poorer outcomes.[41-42]

How to use "self is a social phenomenon" to activate change

 IN SHORT: *Peer context works both ways.*

We care a lot about what other people do. Following the crowd can propel us to act when rational messaging fails. That means: this is one principle that has direct corollaries. If the three levers above can hold people back from making a healthcare decision or trying a new path, they're equally effective in showing the way.

Flipping "keep it cool": Use social signals to show people that change is OK.

People are always looking for social signals; so, why not amplify the most meaningful ones? Whether that's an electric bill showing your home's power usage versus the neighbors', an app that displays your relative time on a run around park, or a public health campaign that shows the relative drop in cigarette smoking in your town, we're always looking for clues that show us where we fit in and what counts as good (enough) behavior. After all, the goal isn't to be perfect. It's just to be on par with or better than most.

In one famous example, Dr. Robert Cialdini, scientific researcher on the psychology of influence, built an intriguing experiment at a hotel. His goal: get more people to reuse their towels. Most hotel guests do reuse their towels at least once, but he was convinced that reuse rates could improve.

To encourage reuse today, most hotels appeal to our sense of doing what's right. Some ask you to save the planet, others offer to plant trees, but all are focused on environmental impact, not the social context. Cialdini simply changed half the signs to tell guests that most of their peers at the hotel, over the course of their stay, reused their towels at least once. Compared with those who saw some message about saving planet Earth, guests who learned that the majority of other guests had reused their towels were 26 percent more likely to recycle their towels. That's a 26 percent increase in participation relative to the industry standard, and it was achieved simply by changing a few words on a sign to convey what others were doing and provide a social signal.[43]

Flipping "deprioritize possibilities": Create transparency to same-role behaviors.

Use social signals to show people what others just like them tend to do to help them align new behaviors with the social roles and identities they care about.

In a Duke University study, researchers told a group of donors to a philanthropic website that the charity would match their contributions, but only if enough donors that day, either 25, 50, 75, or 100 percent of them, committed to a regular, monthly donation. People in the 75 percent group donated at a much higher rate than the rest, demonstrating as high as a 40 percent increase in pledges to donate on a monthly basis. The conclusion was that the higher number is due to a desire to conform to the social norms of other contributors and not be the cause for the charity to deny matching funds.[44]

Flipping "never wander alone": Use social signals to give people a new guide.

We know credible messengers may inspire us to listen to new direction, and role models may help us learn new behavior by being an inspirational example to emulate. Retailers are increasingly blending the two, using the wisdom of the crowd to point people in the right direction and elevating the voices of their most frequent, credible loyalists. These little nudges and techniques take the ambiguity out of the situation and show users what people like them might do.

For instance, the Amazon.com® platform's Frequently Bought Together feature isn't just a means of upselling. Rather, it puts forth a powerful notion: enough shoppers added an item to their cart for there to be a trend with respect to what items they've piled on top of it. This crowd-derived wisdom suggests a product's desirability as much as it promotes additional purchases.

Even Doctors Gravitate Toward The Wisdom of The Crowd

It's tempting to think that following the crowd is just something that *some* people do, and that it's not something *most* people would do—particularly when it comes to those who are more "rational" than average. Doctors, for instance, are a good example. They are trained to care about scientific evidence – and, given the stakes, you would expect them to prioritize data from clinical trials over what the doctor down the hall is doing.

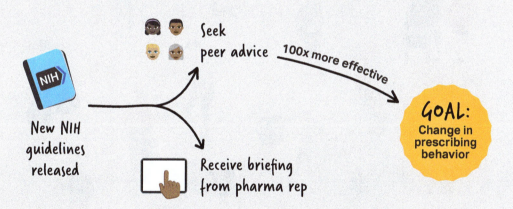

In one study, changes in physicians' prescribing behavior in a particularly serious condition category were examined before and after the release of new NIH practice guidelines for the category. As it turned out, following the guideline release, the prescribing behavior of colleagues who the healthcare provider considered their personal "go-to" for advice was *100 times more influential* on their own subsequent prescribing behavior than the guideline changes they received.[45]

Try this social influence mapping **worksheet** to design interventions that respond to some of the ways we make meaning: ⟶

Social Influence Mapping Worksheet

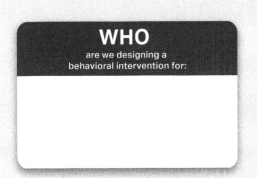

WHO
are we designing a
behavioral intervention for:

Decision moment
that person is at:

What social signals might be interfering with an important healthcare decision or change?

Consider norms and barriers at each of the stakeholder's circles of influence:

Family and Close Friends:
What shared norms might
dictate day-to-day behavior
(think, *we always* or *our way*)?

Community:
What are the rules for interacting,
for information disclosure and for
the availability of support (think,
we talk about or *we expect*)?

Culture:
What are the definitions for how
we think of health, medicine and
wellness (think, *we believe*
or *we fear*)?

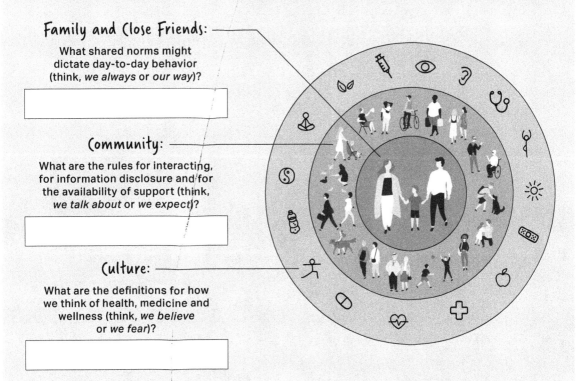

Circle the norms you think are most important to elevate or interrupt. Create ideas for how:

PRINCIPLE 6:

 Goals Organize Our Behavior

THE COMMUNICATOR'S ESSENTIALS:

Goal Role

Goals create focus; they help us choose paths that take us toward our bigger-picture objectives and track progress along the way.

Intention Hierarchy

Goals tend to be organized into three categories: higher-order ambitions, specific objectives and immediate actions.

Goal Formation

One of the most critical elements for healthcare transitions is connecting change to the higher-order goals someone cares about.

Terrible Toos

When setting goals, there are four "toos" that wire us to resist change: too big, too tired, too comfortable, too focused.

Stickiness For Success

To set new goals up for success they need to connect to things we care about, have an action plan, and include micro intentions.

Principle 6: Goals Organize Our Behavior

There's a famous story about an NFL quarterback named Ken O'Brien.[46] When he started in the league, he—surely unintentionally—threw a lot of interceptions. To focus his development, the team wrote a clause into his contract to penalize him for every interception. It worked. His interceptions declined to nearly zero. Of course, that was because he stopped throwing the ball. He had a new goal, after all.

Goals organize our behavior by helping us to stay focused, pick the right path for success, and monitor our progress along the way.

Our goals are very personal, but for the most part, they can be organized in a hierarchy:

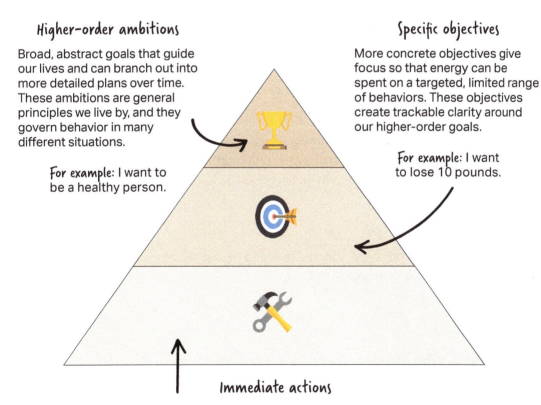

Higher-order ambitions

Broad, abstract goals that guide our lives and can branch out into more detailed plans over time. These ambitions are general principles we live by, and they govern behavior in many different situations.

For example: I want to be a healthy person.

Specific objectives

More concrete objectives give focus so that energy can be spent on a targeted, limited range of behaviors. These objectives create trackable clarity around our higher-order goals.

For example: I want to lose 10 pounds.

Immediate actions

Clear-cut actions and plans are the most tangible example of how goals organize our behavior. They satisfy the higher-order goal and specific objective in a tangible and immediate way.

For example: I want to cut carbs out of my diet.

Goal Formation Is Critical To Healthcare Communications

In healthcare, we invest a lot of time and energy convincing people that it's important to change. But, we know that even when a decision to change has been made, the process of turning that decision into the goals that can help us get started and keep us going is fraught with challenges.

Looking through the lens of behavioral science, one of the most critical shifts we can make as communicators is investing more time in the goal formation process. How can we help people ladder day-to-day change up to the higher-order goals they really care about, the things they believe make them who they are?

That goal formation process is especially critical in three specific circumstances:

1 When people are coming from a previous failure experience (failure of a previous treatment plan, failure to meet a previous goal, etc.).

2 When behavior change needs to be sustained over a long period of time.

3 When behavior change requires a brand-new behavior, like injecting a medicine at home for the first time, or prescribing a new treatment.

Our most important goals are called higher-order goals. Higher-order goals represent our values and aspirational selves. They form important aspects of our identity. Those expressions of what we value and who we strive to be are the ultimate *why* for pursuing our goals. They can help enhance our motivation, especially over the long term. Because these goals are never fully achieved (not satisfied by just one action), they keep us always striving for more.

Higher-order goals give us lots of flexibility in how to pursue them. Going back to the example above, there are many ways to be a healthy person. If that no-carb diet is unsuccessful, everything from meditation to exercise to trying the Noom® weight loss program become new options and actions that act in service of the same *why*.

Why goals can wire us to resist change

 IN SHORT: *Goals can be daunting.*

At times we can unintentionally set unrealistic goals for ourselves. Ones that quickly prove to be difficult to maintain or that have barriers or obstacles that limit our success. But, no matter how difficult or achievable the goal really is, setting and reaching goals is a more complex process than many of us realize. Even well-meaning goals can wire us to resist real change. **We call these types of resistance the Terrible Toos:**

- **Too big:** Without more detailed goal planning, our higher order goals can seem so large or remote that they are virtually inactionable. Those types of goals become so aspirational and out of the every day that they're easy to set aside.

- **Too tired:** The pursuit of goals can require an immense amount of mental energy. It's easy to want to avoid that new tax on our limited resources. This type of resistance is even stronger when the goal setter is worn down by past failures. Those previous defeats can significantly sap energy and motivation.

- **Too comfortable:** We are creatures of habit. A certain inertia sets into our routines. No matter how beneficial we know change will be, the status quo makes us feel good, secure and comfortable. It can be a huge headwind of resistance to setting or acting on a new objective or action.

- **Too focused:** Our commitment to one specific goal or action can prevent us from seeing the need to pivot to a new strategy, one that could ultimately be much more beneficial. Tunnel vision can also lead us to underestimate the time or resources needed to meet the current goal.

How goals can help us activate change:

 IN SHORT: *There are specific ways to set goals up for success.*

Being committed to a goal increases the likelihood that we'll pursue it. But, there are specific ways to design those goals to improve the chances of stickiness and success.

- **Connect to a higher level goal:** Connecting a health behavior to a why or a higher-order goal can change how committed a person is to that goal.

  In one study by researchers at Curtin University, participants were asked to take a multivitamin over a two-week period. Some were asked to think about why that preventative measure was important to them each time they took it. The participants who actively connected the vitamin to a higher-level goal increased their vitamin intake compared to those who were simply following instructions.[47]

- **Create an action plan:** While the higher-order goals tell us why, they don't tell us how. For the *how* we need to form more specific, concrete goals to direct our behavior. More specific goals also help us monitor how we are doing along the way and let us know if we need to pivot.

  Being committed to a goal and creating an action plan increases the likelihood we will pursue it, especially if the goal is complex. How committed we are to that plan depends on a number of variables, including: how important the outcome is to us, our feeling of ownership of the goal, external incentives (e.g. money), and our level of belief that we can achieve it.

- **Develop micro-intentions:** Even with a strong commitment to a goal, we may fail to follow through on the actions we need to take. That kind of failure to execute isn't uncommon in healthcare. Say a person understands why a new treatment has been prescribed and is committed to taking it. She intends to start tomorrow. Except … she never really gets around to it.

That's where micro-intentions or implementation intentions can have a big impact. They bridge the intention-to-action gap by asking people to mentally translate the vague intention of starting a medicine tomorrow into a micro strategy of when, where and how:

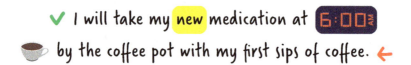

✔ I will take my new medication at 6:00 AM by the coffee pot with my first sips of coffee. ←

Those details form a mental link between a specific aspect of a future situation (drinking my coffee) and the behavior (taking my pill). The act of planning becomes as important – or arguably more important – than the plan itself.

A micro-strategy is even more critical when trying to start a new behavior or when we expect a disruption in our routine, like leaving on a trip, bringing a new baby home, or moving.

These types of micro strategies have been shown to be effective in getting people to follow through on lots of health-related behaviors such as preventive screenings, vaccinations, and keeping follow-up medical appointments.[48-50]

- **Plan for failure:** Wait, not permanent failure. Mistakes will happen and can provide important learning opportunities. Pre-identify ways for them to be seen as pivot points or feedback loops to avoid abandonment of the new goal or routine.

An important part of identifying success or failure is feedback. Initially that feedback should be consistent to set a meaningful baseline. After the first few months, predictable feedback is no longer as useful. It's easy to overlook or to stop paying close attention to it. At that point, feedback should become more variable and unexpected in order to surprise and earn focus.

Diabetes And The Lessons Of Self-Monitoring Fatigue

Feedback is important. It helps us modulate our behavior. But, people get sick of paying attention to themselves. We call it tracking fatigue.

As we help healthcare stakeholders and audiences set goals, the natural inclination is to help them track progress. But, the science is still unsettled on the best way to do that.

Here's an important clue: people living with diabetes have been self-tracking since the 1970s, when doctors asked them to start drawing their own blood at home to measure the level of sugar in it. The readings could point to needed adjustments to diet or medication. The patient became the primary owner of both the monitoring and management of the disease.

A few years ago, researchers asked people with diabetes how they felt about self-monitoring. They said they saw it as the enemy. It undermined their self-esteem and elevated feelings of anxiety and depression.[51] An earlier study found that compliance is incredibly low.[52] Only 5 percent reported monitoring daily, and 65 percent of those on drug therapies reported self-monitoring less than once per month.[52]

Self-monitoring challenges aren't unique to diabetes. It's ongoing work that can feel awkward and create a sense of anxiety or failure. Every self-monitoring strategy needs to be looked at through the lens of what it will feel like at 60 days, 6 months, 6 years, not just right out of the box. With this in mind, we can develop strategies that help people stay aware of important aspects of the condition and their own behavior in ways that don't undercut their motivation.

Try this personal goal planning **worksheet** to understand each of the elements of planning with intention: ⟶

Personal Goal Planning Worksheet

What's one higher-order goal or ambition you have?

Think about something that's connected to how you see yourself or who you want to be.

What's a specific objective that you have against that?

Think about something concrete that you would spend energy against but that likely has multiple steps underneath it.

What's one action you're taking against that objective?

Think about something you could do and track today or tomorrow.

Now, try to create a micro intention against that objective:

I will [what]

at [when]

by [how].

 Good plan. You might want to take a picture of this page!

PRINCIPLE 7:

 Context Is Critical To Our Habits

THE COMMUNICATOR'S ESSENTIALS:

Environmental Factor

The environment we're in can support or limit our ability to change behavior; it consistently primes our thoughts, feelings, and actions.

Subconscious Cues

Habits are routines that are cued by our environment. They're automatic and are triggered by time, location, emotional state, people, and preceding actions.

Context Conundrum

Decision making is not entirely under our direct control—rather, context influences behavior, often without our awareness, through triggers, gaps and competing cues.

Path To Habit

Researchers have identified a consistent loop—a kind of neurological recipe—for how habits are formed and how to change them.

New Plan

Creating a new habit entails creating a new cue that moves you to an action that delivers the reward you're familiar with.

Principle 7: Context Is Critical To Our Habits

If you read *The Tipping Point* by Malcolm Gladwell, you might remember the Power of Context Theory.[53] It revealed how the environment has a much more powerful impact on people's subconscious decisions and behaviors than is generally thought. In fact, many of the decisions or actions that are typically attributed to personal qualities, failures or traits are actually determined by context. Gladwell pointed to big, memorable examples: the mock prison experiment at Stanford that immersed student volunteers in a 24-hour/day prison environment as guards and inmates, and the Bernhard Goetz subway vigilante case in the dirty, crime-ridden New York of the 1980s. He showed that changing the physical and emotional context a group is living in creates a tipping point for real (although not always positive) behavior change.

Context is equally important in personal healthcare decisions and commitments. The environment we're in can either support or limit our ability to engage in a new behavior. We're always responding to hidden cues in our environments. They prime thoughts and feelings and can trigger learned behavior.

Context is critical to how we form habits. Habits are behavioral routines that are cued by our environment. A true habit is automatic and happens outside of our conscious awareness. On the plus side, habits save us a ton of mental energy. On the downside, they are fragile and can be broken if the related environmental cues aren't there.

These habits and reactions are subconscious and almost instantaneous. For example, if someone has often smoked while chatting on the phone, the context of picking up the phone will eventually automatically trigger lighting a cigarette. Or, if you typically scan your phone in bed at night before turning in, eventually just tucking into bed will trigger that subconscious behavior of grabbing your phone and opening Instagram.

Why context and habits can wire us to resist change

 IN SHORT: *Most often, context automatically creates resistance to change.*

Healthcare is largely built on the faulty assumption that all decision-making is under our direct control. That discounts the significant role of environment in creating resistance:

Triggers: Chances are that new habits are being established in exactly the same environment as the old ones. That means everyday triggers – like time of day, location in the home or office, interaction with family or colleagues – are likely to encourage that old habit in a way that makes meaningful change incredibly difficult.

Gaps: Changing environments can create an equally big challenge, especially when it comes to establishing good new habits. In a new environment, all of the context prompts are missing, making sheer will really the only way to perform the behavior. Say, for example, every morning you take a long walk with the family dog right before feeding time. If you're traveling for business or for fun, there's no dog, no feeding time, no environmental cues to take that long walk. Do you still take it?

Competing Cues: Our environments are subtly reminding us to do all sorts of things. Sometimes those habits and priorities compete. New, carefully laid context connections might help you remember to take a medication or to work out, but those new habits could be undermined if watching a favorite program on the couch at night with your significant other prompts you to have a salty snack or a scoop of ice cream.

How context and habits can activate change

 IN SHORT: *Forming new habits follows a consistent path.*

Let's talk about how habits actually work and what role context clues play in them. Researchers at MIT's McGovern Institute for Brain Research have identified a fairly consistently loop—or neurological recipe—for habits.[54]

It starts with a routine. Say every night after work you come home, pour a glass of wine, and talk about the day with your spouse on the porch. Pretty nice routine, but it most often means no time to exercise before dinner, and the pounds are starting to creep on.

The routine is the behavior you want to change.

Now, we have to figure out: what is the context cue and what is the reward? In his book *The Power of Habit*, Charles Duhigg points to a framework to dig into your routine.[55]

If context is the prompt for a habit, rewards are its fuel. They satisfy cravings we may not even be aware we have.

What's the real reward here? Is it unstructured time to unwind? Attention from a significant other? A little buzz from a glass of wine? Something else entirely? This is the real challenge of diagnosing a reward in either a real life or market research setting: it's largely a matter of generating and testing hypotheses.

One night, you might try taking a leisurely walk with your significant other instead of having a glass of wine. Another you might try having tea instead of wine. Or just going to work out or meditate entirely alone, trying new hypotheses until you uncover what the real underlying habit-forming reward is.

After each experiment, write down your reactions. How do you feel? What happened? Any loose associations will help you capture your thoughts. Then wait. After a few minutes do you still feel a desire for the habit you missed? If you do, you haven't isolated what you're actually craving.

Let's say, in this case, we've isolated that the reward is unstructured time—a moment with no specific next tasks to complete. Now, let's uncover the context cue.

We can classify most habit-forming cues as one of five types: location, time, emotional state, other people, preceding action.[55] Let's ask those questions:

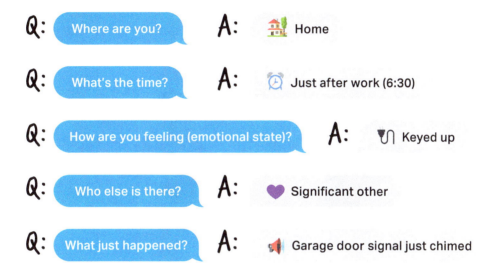

This exercise should be repeated over a number of days to look for patterns. Eventually, you might find that the trigger is those days when you leave work feeling keyed up or simply the time of day when you need a break between work and real life.

From there, you're in a position to make a plan. One that delivers the reward (unstructured time) and responds to the cue (time of day). A plan might look like putting the dog leash out in the morning and grabbing both pet and significant other for a walk that delivers that unstructured time. New cue, new routine, same reward.

For ease of understanding, much of this information has been put in personal context: how you might diagnose the context and reward cues of a habit. To design healthcare communications and interventions, this same process informs an incredibly valuable observational research technique that seeks experimentally to understand the real-life elements of a habit.

Try this habit map **worksheet** to evaluate what rewards and cues might be driving your stakeholder's negative health habits. How will they help you design interventions that leverage context clues for success? ⟶

Habit Map Worksheet

WHO
are we designing a behavioral intervention for:

Healthcare Professional

Patient

What habit do we want to interrupt?

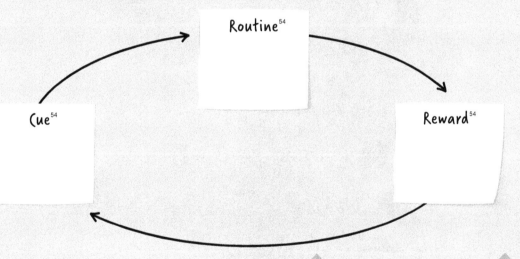

Routine[54]

Cue[54]

Reward[54]

 What does that routine look like today?
_____

 What are your hypotheses about what the rewards are for that routine?
_____
_____
_____

 What are your hypotheses about what the cues are? Remember, most habit-forming cues fall into one of five categories: location, time, emotional state, other people, preceding action.[55]
_____

Circle your top hunch for which is the most likely reward and the most likely cue.

Now, design a new plan.

What will give people that reward with a healthier behavior? What context cue can you remove or interrupt to short-circuit the existing habit? What context cue could you add to promote the new habit?

_____
_____
_____

PRINCIPLE 8:

 We Constantly Redefine Normal

THE COMMUNICATOR'S ESSENTIALS:

Simply Settling

We think of resilience primarily as a positive coping mechanism, but what's abnormal can quickly start to feel normal – even when it shouldn't.

Low Dissatisfaction

We can come to accept a lower quality of health by satisficing: making decisions that suffice and satisfy rather than optimize.

Low Hope

Anchor points can make it difficult for us to imagine a present that doesn't include lower expectations or limited quality of life.

New Normal

To set a new normal, it's important to provide benchmarks that can help people understand what they control and set new goals.

Fresh Start

Big life events create catalytic moments to reset expectations and pursue a better quality of life and health.

Principle 8: We Constantly Redefine Normal

When it comes to our health, what's abnormal can quickly start to feel normal.

Let's throw a big behavioral science term at you: Hedonic Adaptation.[56] Sounds like a great one, right? You should definitely use it in a meeting. It's an important process that's hardwired into all of us. We get used to changes in life experiences. When a significant injury happens – loss of mobility, loss of a loved one – people are eventually able to return to a relatively stable baseline of happiness. The opposite is true, too. When a significant gain happens – new salary, new gadget – the excitement wanes and we return to that same baseline.

Some experts call it the hedonic treadmill. There are theories that you can get "boosts" on that treadmill with smaller positive experiences (like exercise or religious practices) that advance progress back to that stable baseline of happiness.[57]

Getting used to life experiences can be a good thing or a bad thing. Often, the difference between the two is a person's store of resilience.

Imagine Person 1. She's in a tragic accident. She loses part of her left leg. After months of physical therapy, she walks with a prosthetic. After years of training, she runs a half marathon. She's healthier and more active than she was before the accident. She had a huge swell of resilience, measured by not just the physical rebound but also by the ability to adapt psychologically. Resilience is the ability to bounce back from disappointment, fight off overwhelming feelings of emotional pain, and find the determination needed to carry on and redefine what it means to live life to the fullest. It's the psychological fuel that gets her to that finish line. Every day there are millions of examples of people creating their new normal in the face of adversity.

Imagine Person 2. Over time, walking has become more difficult. Pain in her left knee and hip slow her down. She believes she'll never have the same mobility again; so, she mostly stays home, uses a motorized cart when she goes to the grocery and has told friends and family she can't do her usual activities. She may be adapting and working around the realities of her current condition. But, if she has lost hope that she can enjoy life in spite of her limitations and lacks the confidence that she can make any improvements to her situation, she can get stuck in a demotivating cycle of emotional distress and resignation. Her new normal could be holding her back from asking the questions that could improve her health situation or quality of life even in small ways.

Why (too) easily adapting to a new normal can wire us to resist change

 IN SHORT: *Lack of resilience can keep us from needed help and support.*

Resilience is important, because behavior change isn't smooth and linear. It's bumpy and takes lots of twists and turns. When learning new behavior, we need to go through trial and error and not give up when we make mistakes. Even once behavior is learned, lots of things can get in our way of following through (e.g. a bad day, a business trip, a family crisis). If we succumb to feelings of guilt or disappointment, we can easily give up on our aspirations and goals. Resilience is what helps us bounce back from disruption, learn from our mistakes, and get ourselves back on track.

Like our Person 2 above, people may find it difficult to pursue positive healthcare change. They take critical health warning signs and translate them with resignation into something they'll simply have to live with. For instance, someone might think, "I guess if I throw up every day, that's my new normal." Whew, we hope not.

The drivers of resistance are all connected to the way that novelty (of even negative situations) wears off and how quickly we lower our expectations for the future.

Low dissatisfaction: When we come to accept – even expect – lower quality of life or health, it's easy to "satisfice." That means making decisions that satisfy and suffice rather than optimize. People have an incredible ability to adapt, but that might mean they are putting up with very difficult symptoms, lack of improvement, or complex treatment routines. That may lower their motivation to seek better options (even when knowing that there is something new out there).

Low hope: We don't give up on anchoring points easily. Once centered on believing that, to extend the example, limited mobility is part of aging, it becomes difficult to imagine a future that doesn't include those lowered expectations for what day-to-day life can be like. As we design interventions, we need to share meaningful benchmarks and make it clear that in many cases *better* is achievable and worth investing in.

How (too) easily adapting to a new normal can activate change

 IN SHORT: *The attributes of positive resilience can help us cope.*

We have an incredible ability to adapt to our circumstances and cope in the face of adversity. Resilience, that power to bounce back from disruption, can also get us back on the path of behavior change.

What do resilient people have in common? They do five things:

1 Know what they can control

2 Think positively

3 See and address challenges

4 Don't blame themselves

5 Act on goals

Those five things can point to a path for behavioral design that helps people adapt to disruption and establish a new normal without feeling – or getting – defeated.

- **Know what they can control:** Can we leverage benchmarks and peer experience to show people where their locus of control and ability to change really sits?

- **Think positively:** Are there ongoing prompts and feedback loops that can help users recognize achievement and progress? That can give them reason for hope and keep realistic optimism alive?

- **See and address challenges:** What potential issues can we actively anticipate users having? Are there frictions or barriers we can move out of the way? How can we help them plan their comeback strategy?

- **Don't blame themselves:** How can we give people permission to learn from their missteps and get back on track with confidence?

- **Act on goals:** Can we use what we learned in Principle 6 (Goals Organize Our Behavior) to help people set goals connected to their higher-order ambitions?

The Fresh Start Effect

Big life events can be the perfect time to pursue change. They create a moment to reconsider previous decisions and can even shift how we think about ourselves.

A **new** job, **new** city, and **new** relationship can all be moments of powerful resilience and change.

But so, too, can little events. As little as, say, next Monday. Researchers have found that among a cohort of university students, the likelihood of committing to a new gym habit increases at "fresh start" moments like the beginning of a new week, month, or semester.[58]

Try this resilience **worksheet** to evaluate how to pull levers on both sides of the positive / negative adaptation equation: ⟶

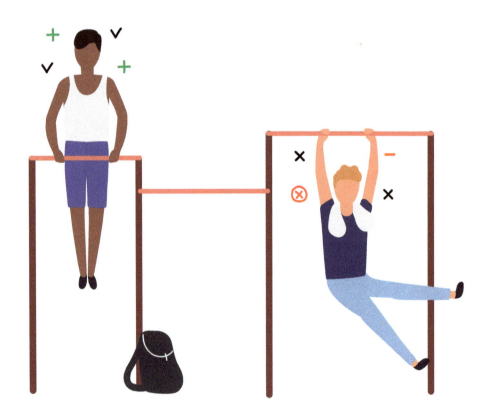

Resilience Worksheet

 What health challenge do we want to address?

Simply Settling

 What are people accepting that they don't have to?

 In what ways are they satisficing?

 What benchmarks or new interventions might win them back and make them reconsider that new normal?

Fueling Resilience

 What can people control / what can't they control?

 What should they be prepared for as they make this change? What challenges might present themselves?

 How can we support them to think positively and keep moving forward?

Circle your top two interventions. What would it take to execute them?

Intervention

Execution Questions and Needs

PRINCIPLE 9:

 Motivation Is Fleeting

THE COMMUNICATOR'S ESSENTIALS:

Leaky Bucket

No matter how excited and determined we are at the start of a behavior change journey, that store of motivation quickly drips away and needs constant replenishment.

Motivation Recipe

Three types of expectations determine if we will cross the bridge from intent to action: benefit expectations, effort expectations and ability expectations.

Impact of Time

A person's ability to self-motivate and forge on decline over time, especially when the behavior hasn't become a habit and barriers persist.

Depleting Forces

We aren't good at monitoring our own buckets of motivation. We tend to overestimate our own willpower and underestimate the forces that are depleting it.

Resilience Builders

We can help close the holes in the leaky bucket of motivation by bringing the future forward, giving new rewards and amplifying the *why* behind behavior change.

Principle 9: Motivation Is Fleeting

Behavioral scientists talk about motivation as a leaky bucket. No matter how completely you are able to fill that bucket in one powerful communication or through one meaningful intervention, it quickly starts to drip away, losing a little through one hole (confidence), more through another (attention), and another (ability). Soon, what once felt catalytic is practically forceless.

We can't just turn interest on and trust that it will stay on. Our job is to constantly refill the bucket. We have to create the context and consistent support that will turn that interest to commitment; commitment to action; and action to resilience.

Let's step back and talk about some of the basic drivers that create motivation. Those things that help us cross the bridge from intent to action in order to start or change a behavior.

The motivation recipe essentially has three ingredients: benefits + effort + ability

Benefit Expectations:
What advantage will the person receive by taking the action? Those benefits could include anything from an ability to regain something lost to creating new skills to changing perceptions about oneself. 
Effort Expectations:
What effort will the task take? The type of work it could take might be functional, emotional or social. Meaning, it might cost money, require an embarrassing conversation, and maybe even create conflict with a family dynamic. Ultimately, belief that the benefit of the change will outweigh the costs will help drive change.
Ability Expectations:
Can the person do this? That question isn't purely about ability; it's also about confidence. People have to believe they have the internal capacity and external resources to be successful. That internal capacity includes knowledge, skills and psychological stamina. Ability is a really important aspect of motivation in healthcare. Even if your message is compelling and top of mind, it may not be something people believe they can do. For example, they may not feel confident that they can ask their doctor pointed questions about treatment. In some cases, they may not have the skills to open that conversation in an effective way. They may not realize they lack those skills until well after they've heard that message and are trying to turn their motivation into action.

Once that first action is taken, the motivation equation changes somewhat. It becomes more connected to alignment, satisfaction and enjoyment. In other words, in order to maintain motivation, the new behavior has to align with how the person thinks of herself; the effort needs to feel worth the outcome; and the behavior has to be enjoyable (or at least not horrible! This is still healthcare).

Even under these conditions, though, we know that a person's ability to forge on often declines with time. That is especially true under conditions in which the behavior hasn't become an ingrained habit and requires persistent effort to overcome barriers. In those situations, so much hinges on nurturing and sustaining motivation.

Why the leaky bucket wires us to resist change

 **IN SHORT:** *We overestimate people's willpower and underestimate everything that is constantly depleting the bucket of motivation.*

However impactful a message might be, people's motivation is often fleeting. That can even be true when the healthcare message you're talking about is important to people and they're highly invested in it. That starts to make sense when you think about what it takes for people to act on their intentions. What follows are just some of the headwinds to maintaining motivation:

First, life is busy.

We're constantly juggling multiple priorities and can act on only a few at a time. Between receiving a healthcare message and when we can really act on it, all kinds of things drop in and divert motivation and intention to all kinds of other things we want or need to accomplish. Folding the laundry can win out over emailing your doctor about a new treatment option in almost any household.

Competing pressures aren't all immediate. There is also tension between short- and long-term goals. Long-term goals, like being healthier or getting a condition under control, are abstract, distant and tend to be uncertain. Short-term goals have lots of in-the-moment detail. They're concrete and tend to have more certain outcomes. Because they're both attainable and urgent, they're easier for our brains to get hooked on.

Even the same decision can have different outcomes on different timelines. Say your doctor's office calls to schedule your annual physical. The first appointment available is two months from now. That decision is likely to be made based on abstracts, like wanting to stay healthy and doing a better job of keeping up with preventative care. What about when the first opening is tomorrow morning due to another patient's canceling? Now, your decision making is much more concrete and competitive with short-term considerations. There's the traffic, the logistics with work or childcare, the time you'd have to get up, and all the other details that now stand in stark relief to moving forward.

Temptation is everywhere.

Our desire to self-satisfy by doing something other than the right thing can be, well, very tempting. There are actually three reasons behind that – each decodes a different aspect of human behavior:

1. **Craving.** Once we've started to think about a temptation, our brain knows something good is about happen. That "good" we actually feel as a kind of stress. The fastest way to relieve that stress: indulge the craving.

2. **Scarcity.** When we perceive a shortage of something, we want it more. We fixate our attention on it and prioritize that short-term reward over long-term goals. For example, if you've given up salty and processed foods to help control hypertension, the fact that you can't have those foods might leave you with the feeling of constantly being deprived. To avoid them requires a consistently high level of motivation.

3. **Exhaustion.** Our self-control is easily exhausted, and that makes us vulnerable to doing the exact opposite of what we intended to do. The ability to inhibit competing impulses, control our emotions, and keep going on difficult tasks is part of a process called self-regulation. It helps us complete purposeful goals. It also takes a ton of energy. Often, we aren't even aware that we are exhausted and vulnerable to failing.

We lose the why.

This aspect of resistance is particularly important to long-term adherence to a medical treatment or lifestyle change. To stick with behavior change, we have to see the outcomes as worth the effort exerted. We have to believe – week to week, year to year – that it's worth it. That benefit and the *why* behind our original intent and commitment can get lost over time. As symptoms start to improve or overall health plateaus, it can be easy for doubt to creep in: *Do I really need this? Is the condition really that severe?*

That doubt creep can be especially powerful for people who have silent conditions with no symptoms (like high blood pressure). They're asked to trudge on with treatment and health regimens that have no external signals of benefit or value. The occasional test results or physician check-ins are remote from their everyday routine.

How we can use the holes in the leaky bucket to activate change

IN SHORT: *Each of the levers of resistance is also a lever of change.*

Because the holes in the leaky bucket are so well defined, we can design communications and interventions to address them specifically and give people more of what they need to try and try again.

From: Life Is Busy → To: Bring the Future Forward

We can design interventions and communications that prompt people to think about the future in order to align today's behavior with their future preferences. Some emerging research shows how visual techniques that help people see how they will look in the future might tap into those future rewards and/or consequences. A recent paper written by Hal E. Hershfield at New York University brought together theoretical and empirical work to suggest that we're best able to make long-term choices that will benefit our future selves when the image or idea we create of the future self shares similarities with the present self, is seen in vivid and realistic terms and, importantly, is seen in a positive light.[59]

To ease that life-is-busy burden, we can also communicate shorter-term impacts and consequences while actively working to minimize the "cost" side of the equation and reminding people how easy it can be to create change in their own lives.

From: Temptation is Everywhere → To: Give New Rewards

Feeding a craving feels good. Other rewards can feel good, too. Long-term gains are a long way off, but small rewards received along the way can help create momentum, reinforcing behavior change and helping people to progress to greater change and lasting habits.

Those rewards could be intrinsic if we can show short-term impact against physical aspects of health and wellbeing or progress toward a larger health goal. They could also be extrinsic, like financial incentives, check-ins from a healthcare professional or advocate, or interim test results.

Using External Rewards To Fill The Bucket

Wouldn't it be simpler if we could just pay people to change? Money can be a powerful motivator, after all. But is it powerful enough for real change?

A number of experiments and studies have shown the short-term impact of financial incentives. From gift cards for mammograms to perks for showing up for follow-up, there have been meaningful signals of impact.[60] But longer-term research shows those incentives aren't as sticky or motivating over time.

For example, the Affordable Care Act granted 10 states a total of $85 million to pilot programs that would provide financial rewards as part of a total strategy to reduce the risk of chronic disease in Medicaid populations. Over five years, the states launched programs in diabetes prevention, weight management, and smoking cessation. California gave gift cards and nicotine replacement therapy to people who were willing to ask for support on the state's smoking cessation line. Minnesota offered reward payments to patients who completed a diabetes prevention class and got updated bloodwork. The early results showed that people were more likely to participate in preventative activities. An evaluation of these programs showed that incentives helped persuade people to pursue prevention.[61]

But, a final report by the Center on Budget and Policy Priorities said, the results of similar pilots have been mixed.[62] The incentive programs can help people make short-term change, like choosing to attend a class or stick with an appointment. But they're less likely to drive lasting change, like weight loss. Worse, the report said that sometimes those incentives are going to people who would have exhibited the healthy behavior anyway.

From: We Lose the Why → To: Amplify The Why

Making an internal commitment to change is important, but introducing a social factor can supercharge that commitment. Healthcare interventions that help people both connect change to their higher-order goals and actively communicate their *why* to a friend or family member can both amplify motivation and keep that *why* at the forefront. The person making the commitment not only has to talk out loud about why—they now also have someone waiting to hear about their progress.

Try this balance **worksheet** to uncover new ways you can fill that leaky bucket of motivation. ⟶

Balance Sheet Worksheet

What health change do we want someone to make or keep?

Briefly describe the person we're asking to make that change.
Think: what context is impacting them (life, health, family, education, income, etc.)

What does the balance of benefit, effort and ability look like for that person and that change?

Benefit Expectations

What advantage will the person receive by taking the action?

Effort Expectations

What effort will the task take?

Ability Expectations

Can the person do this? What skills or barriers might be in the way?

How does the balance sheet look? Do the benefits outweigh the effort required and any gaps in ability?

If yes, will that stay the same over time? ☐ Yes ☐ No

If the balance is off, how can you use the approaches in this chapter to activate or sustain change?

Idea 1

Idea 2

Idea 3

Our "Gut" Can Deceive Us

When we create interventions and communications to help people make more informed healthcare decisions or commit to change, we're playing a really important role in overcoming the predictable ways that these principles of behavioral science deceive us and make us believe that something is obvious, when it really isn't at all.

Try this: Which line is longer?

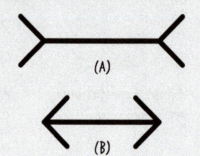

(A)

(B)

They're the same length. But every signal you're getting is that the top one is longer. We need to interrupt those signals that are routinely sending people to the wrong answers.

The Behavior Brief

Q: What can your organization do to reduce or eliminate those barriers and challenges to help more people confidently make the best healthcare decisions for themselves?

The behavior brief asks teams to think about those questions through the lens of the 9 Principles of Influence. Each principle has a core question to answer to form a complete picture of the behavioral design needed to optimize a healthcare communication or program.

No one principle is the answer in itself. Instead, the most effective way to get people to change is combining the most relevant principles as levers of change.

That combination of principles will vary based on the health issue or decision you're addressing. Start by selecting the 3–4 principles you think are most critical to engaging your unique audience. Then, answer the questions to find new ways to break through the barriers to change and give people more motivation and resilience in the face of health challenges.

Example:

Q: *What core needs does the health condition or treatment violate?*

Need for variety...

∿ The 9 Principles of Influence ∿

Principle 1: Core emotional needs drive us

Q: *What core needs does the health condition or treatment violate?*

Principle 2: Mental processing is limited

Q: *What could make this decision or change feel overwhelming?*

Principle 3: Irrational shortcuts guide decision making

Q: *What cognitive biases are people likely bringing to this decision?*

Principle 4: We understand the present through the past

Q: *What past experiences could be impacting openness or ability to change?*

Principle 5: Self is a social phenomenon

Q: *What social norms and influences might impact this decision or change?*

Principle 6: Goals organize our behavior

Q: *What higher order goals could this change or decision align to?*

Principle 7: Context is critical to our habits

Q: *What triggers, gaps and competing cues might prevent a person from building a new habit?*

Principle 8: We constantly redefine normal

Q: *What limitations or health risks are people accepting today that they don't have to?*

Principle 9: Motivation is fleeting

Q: *What can we do to continue to fill the leaky bucket of motivation and give people resilience to try and try again?*

Part 2: The (Behavioral) Science of Segmenting

The 9 Principles of Influence will help any team design healthcare communications and programs that are responsive to what causes people to resist change. These principles help us think beyond the benefit of a new procedure, treatment or health behavior to the real-life context that change has to happen in. As a colleague of ours once said, "it doesn't matter if the benefit is life-*saving* if you don't believe you can do it. And, in most cases, we're just talking about incrementally life improving. The bar for action is higher than you think."

The 9 Principles are what we all have in common. They are shared truths about being human, although each of us experiences them in slightly different ways.

In the era of omni-channel communications, we don't have to stop at just what we have in common. We can further segment communications and experiences to get closer and closer to each individual's personal source of identity and motivation.

In this short section, we want to introduce what those kinds of segmentation schemas could look like. Ones that are based on a user's data or actions and can quickly take them to more and more relevant content.

Segmentation schemas can get complex. But, they don't have to be. We selected three examples of incredibly powerful behavioral dichotomies that simply bifurcate your audience: some are more like this / the others are more like that.

To use a simple analogy, let's say, half prefer the New England Patriots and half prefer the Pittsburgh Steelers. If we were treating the entire addressable audience the same, we would simply say they enjoy football. Perhaps, professional football to be more specific. But, once we know a person prefers the Steelers, there are much more rallying, inciting and motivating connections we can make that go way beyond the general sport or even the League.

To know who is who, we can use actions or data.

Actions are, in short, what a person chooses to invest attention in. Something as simple as a digital ad can help people self-segment. Let's continue with the sports example to see what that might look like. Say we are marketing a snack brand. One ad might mention watching the Steelers playoff with a big bag of [snack]. The other might mention watching the Patriots dynasty with a big bag of [snack]. That's a straightforward choice: you'll most likely click on the one you feel a team affiliation with; from there, we can easily customize the rest of the messaging, website or follow-up to include your favorite team.

Data works in a more predictive way. Models can be created to spot the different digital locations each sport fan is most likely to be in leveraging a combination of geography, social behavior and search data.

Okay, enough sports. Back to healthcare.

Behavioral science lets us go beyond those shared human truths to starting to categorize people by how those truths are manifested in their own lives. Researchers have found patterns that can categorize how people look at the world, how they process information, and how they respond. We'll take a look at three in this section:

Promoter / Preventer

Individualism / Collectivism

Locomotion / Assessment

Understanding these segments will let us identify critical conversation shifts that power customized consumer pathways with content, support and experience.

Promoter / Preventer

When it comes to communication, 25 years of research has shown that people are motivated one of two ways: promoter or preventer.[63-64]

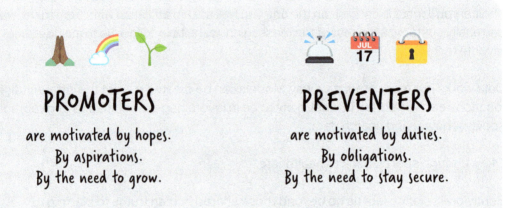

PROMOTERS
are motivated by hopes.
By aspirations.
By the need to grow.

PREVENTERS
are motivated by duties.
By obligations.
By the need to stay secure.

Imagine how different the conversation would have to be to motivate those two distinctly different styles. If you tell a preventer "Ask about the medication. Live your best life!" you instantly lose their trust and interest. Sources of motivation and persistence are incredibly personal. And every word matters.

Let's dig a little further into each of the motivational styles:

A PROMOTER

is someone who:

 Sees their goals as ideals that they aspire to accomplish

 Is focused on seeking gains or making progress toward their goals

 Feels elated when things go right, and sad when things go wrong

 Is open to change and exploring options

 Finds it easy to think in broad, sweeping terms

 Feels like the future is something they can see clearly

 Takes risks when they think it'll maximize expected value

Promoters like imagery that involves the big picture. They prefer messages that are about eagerly achieving good outcomes rather than ones that are about vigilantly avoiding negative outcomes. They like to hear their goals described in terms of hopes and dreams to which they can aspire. And they're open to experiences that involve novelty and variety.

A PREVENTER

is someone who:

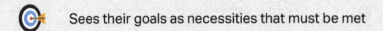 Sees their goals as necessities that must be met

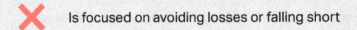 Is focused on avoiding losses or falling short

Feels anxious when things go wrong, and at peace when things go right

Prefers the trees over the forest – because the devil is in the details

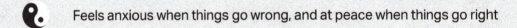 Prefers the status quo, and likes to work on things one at a time

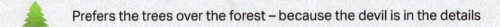 Is focused on the here and now

Takes risks when it's a matter of "doing what's necessary"

Preventers like concrete details and experiences, as opposed to abstract, big-sky ideas.

They prefer messages that are about vigilantly avoiding negative outcomes rather than ones that are about eagerly achieving good outcomes. They like to hear their goals described in terms of the things that involve maintaining safety and security. And they prefer experiences that they can persist with that don't involve multitasking.

For healthcare, we've customized these categories slightly to reflect the unique journey of life and health. We call them achievers (built from the promoter persona) and defenders (built from the preventer persona). A short quiz can help you uncover your motivational style and learn more about how the segment like you engages with healthcare information.

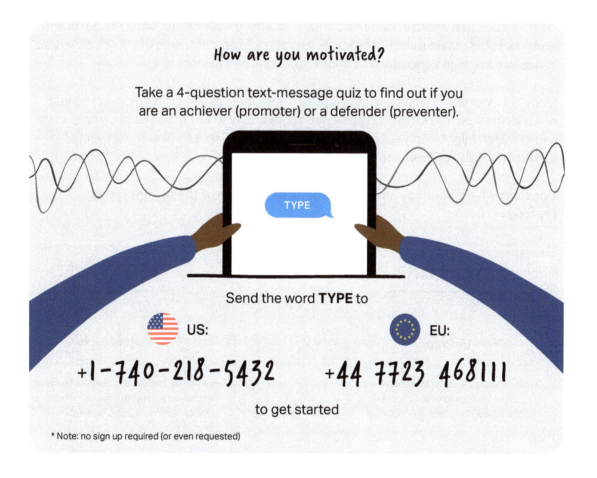

In omnichannel programs, these underlying insights are leveraged to create responsive consumer pathways. Distinct messages and content are written to appeal to preventers and promoters separately. Based on the content they respond to, they're taken to more and more motivational style–customized experiences with each tap or click.

Individualism / Collectivism

Individualism vs. Collectivism is a typology and segmenting method based upon fundamental differences in the way people see themselves relative to their social group.[65] It tends to track with certain group differences, such as those between Eastern and Western cultures.[66-67]

In healthcare, that mindset becomes critical to what influences us, what drives us and even what sources we trust. For example, it can be a key determinant of the effectiveness of health campaign concepts that appeal to values and identity.[68]

Many behavioral scientists see individualism and collectivism existing on something of a sliding scale. You might find audience segments who firmly sit in one camp or data and research might lead you to more nuanced grouping that have some attributes in individualism and others in collectivism.

Consider where your key audience groups sit on each of these important typology criteria:

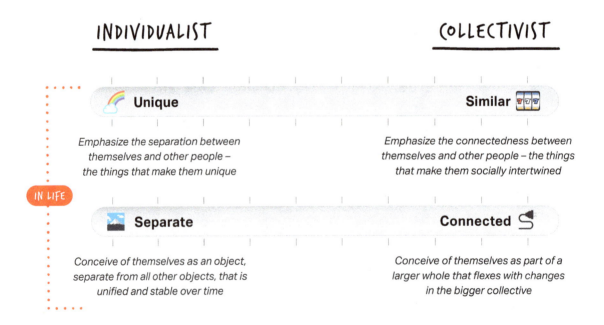

INDIVIDUALIST

COLLECTIVIST

Unique

Emphasize the separation between themselves and other people – the things that make them unique

Similar

Emphasize the connectedness between themselves and other people – the things that make them socially intertwined

IN LIFE

Separate

Conceive of themselves as an object, separate from all other objects, that is unified and stable over time

Connected

Conceive of themselves as part of a larger whole that flexes with changes in the bigger collective

INDIVIDUALIST

COLLECTIVIST

 **In Control**

In Context

 IN LIFE

Focus on, and attribute their behavior to, their personal abilities, beliefs, attitudes, and goals– and gain self-esteem when their behavior expresses those personal characteristics

Focus on their social statuses, roles, and relationships, and attribute their behavior to the requirements of social situations and context. Gain self-esteem when they successfully fit in

 Self-Reliant

Dependent

Rely on their inner preferences for making health decisions

Look to their inner circle to understand what their health preferences should be

➡ **Direct**

Indirect ♂

Tend to speak directly to Healthcare professionals about their experiences and desires

Tend to speak to doctors in passive, indirect voice

 IN HEALTH

 Self-Led

Expert-Led

Need the right skills and beliefs (e.g., self-efficacy) that empower self-directed action

Defer to doctors and their inner circle for treatment decisions

🏅 **Goal-Oriented**

Trust-Oriented

Benefit from tools and tips that support individual initiative in health behavior

May prefer messages from authoritative in-group figures that stress harmony with the broader group

Healthcare Professionals Can Be Segmented
By Individualism / Collectivism, Too

INDIVIDUALIST HEALTHCARE PROFESSIONALS MAY:

 Expect their patients to share their own take-charge mindset

 Overestimate the willpower patients bring to health self-management

 Focus on a patient's responsibility for managing health

 Assume that the behavior they see (e.g. engagement or nonadherence) defines who the patient is

 Misinterpret patients' cues about their internal beliefs and feelings

 Put a premium on standing out from professional peers

COLLECTIVIST HEALTHCARE PROFESSIONALS MAY:

 Feel it is important to bring family into conversations and seek consensus

 Be less likely to blame patients for their health behavior

 Modulate how they communicate to best fit the patient

 Pick up on subtle signs of distress or unstated needs

 Tune into the external forces that might be influencing patients' abilities to manage their health

 Feel it is important to be seen as keeping in step with the norms and expectations of their peers

Locomotion / Assessment

We should note first that the locomotion-assessment is the least explored within current literature. But it does start to point to some provocative and powerful cues for healthcare segmentation.

The dichotomy was initially developed under the name Regulatory Mode Theory by E. Tory Higgins and Arie Kruglanski.[69-70] The two were interested in goal pursuit and motivation. They believe that locomotion and assessment represent the two key ways people approach situations to achieve a goal. People who are more locomotive are focused on getting things done. People who are more assessment-oriented will compare different goals and analyze different options.

Here's how the two segments break down and how to appeal to each:

Locomotion	Assessment
Focus primarily on forward movement and getting on with it	Focus primarily on fully sizing things up so as to understand their value or utility
De-emphasize the value of scrutinizing their goals, their choice options, or the means they use to move ahead	Prioritize such activities as comparing choice options attribute by attribute, examining how well certain courses of action have performed in the past, etc.
Zero in on a small set of top priority attributes to make go/no-go decisions and skip comparisons to other options	Spend a lot of time mulling over attributes of treatment options, and keep searching for information before deciding
Likely abandon a treatment or service if methods of use are too complex to quickly routinize	Likely abandon a treatment or service if they have a negative experience with it (e.g., an adverse event) and believe that other alternatives could have been pursued
Potentially quickly onboard with treatment once they are "bought in," assuming no logistical obstacles (e.g., over-complexity that breaks flow)	Likely procrastinate before onboarding onto a treatment or adopting a health behavior

Understanding the differences between Locomotion and Assessment styles helps to quickly identify what kinds of content and communications will be most relevant as well as to time the triggers and reminders according to likely decision velocity.

Conclusion

Go back to page 14. Were you able to achieve your goals through the book? Did you validate your hypotheses or challenge them? Did you develop any new understandings of your customer or healthcare stakeholders?

That's what behavioral science does: help us see people more clearly and understand the subconscious ways we either help ourselves move forward or hold ourselves back. It opens doors to change.

Let us share one last story. It's about cholera, when it was still a raging epidemic.

In the 1800s, cholera rolled over the city of London every few years. In 1854, an outbreak tore through the SoHo neighborhood and killed 10 percent of the population in 10 days.

No one knew what was causing it, but the prevailing wisdom (the miasma theory) was that it was in the air, which in 1800s London was a noxious vapor of human waste, garbage and industry. Many already believed the air was bad; it wasn't a far leap to conclude that it was deadly.

Of course, we now know that cholera was in the water. We know that because of John Snow.

In the middle of the outbreak, Snow, a local doctor, started knocking on doors to map who had died at what address. He used that data to build a map—a ghost map—that marked the number of people who died at each address with little black lines.

What you see on the map is a pronounced cluster of deaths right around 40 Broad St. – a popular water pump. Ah-ha: cholera is a water-borne disease. Snow convinces the authorities of his theory. They remove the pump handle and the epidemic stops. They invest in infrastructure projects – like the London sewers – to clean up the water. And just over a decade later, cholera is gone from London forever. A page-turning triumph of science.

Except that almost everything about the way we know the John Snow story is wrong.

Steven Johnson researched the ghost map in detail and uncovered the parts of the story that history has largely forgotten.[71-72] Snow had the theory that cholera was a water-borne disease for six years before cholera came to SoHo. He wrote papers, published letters to the editors, made other maps. He had ideas. He had the message and the facts; he just couldn't drive behavior change.

At the time of the SoHo outbreak, Snow had found a collaborator: Henry Whitehead, a local vicar. Whitehead was a classic connector who knew everyone in the neighborhood. He knew what they cared about, worried about and needed in the face of this terrible epidemic.

Whitehead used that unique understanding of real people to open doors in SoHo that Snow never could. He used his close relationships with local families to help Snow gather the individual narratives about the disease that would corroborate his theory after public health officials initially rejected it. He connected Snow to grieving people outside of SoHo, in otherwise healthy communities, where Snow learned that their infirm and deceased loved ones had traveled to the Broad Street pump—thus creating Snow's decision-driving map.

If we leave you with one thought, it's this: the message isn't enough. No matter how compelling the science, how clear the benefit, it's not enough if you don't understand the people. What motivates them. What gives them hope. That's what opens doors and keeps them open for the hard conversations, new understandings, and big commitments to change.

This is our opportunity to design healthcare communications differently.

Puzzle solutions

Solution 1.

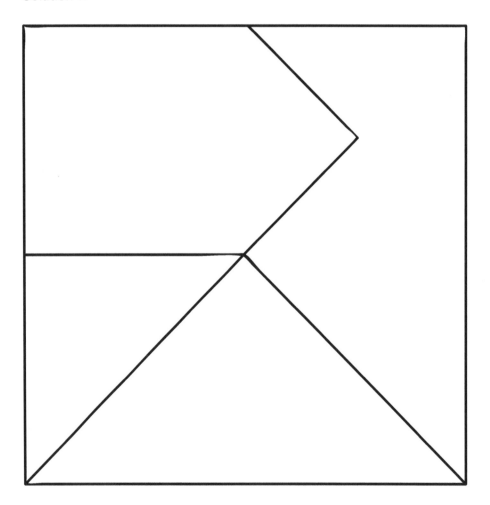

Solution 2.

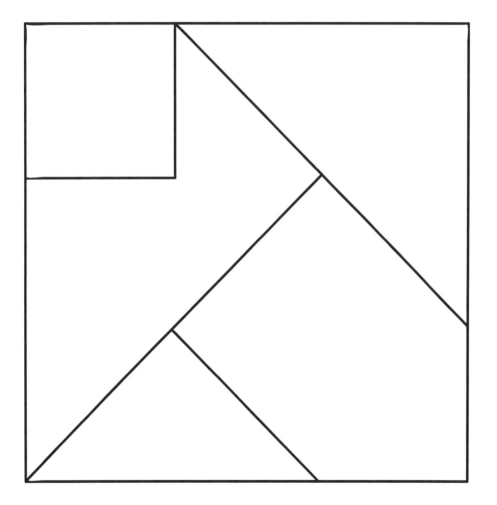

References and Citations

1. Choi J. The nature of science: an activity for the first day of class. Summer Research Program for Science Teachers. Scienceteacherprogram.org. Web site: http://www.scienceteacherprogram.org/genscience/Choi04.html. Published August 2004. Accessed March 2, 2019.

2. Weisberg J, Gladwell M. Malcolm gladwell's 12 rules for life Season 3 Episode 7. Revisionist History. http://revisionisthistory.com/episodes/27-malcolm-gladwell-s-12-rules-for-life. Accessed July 2, 2019.

3. Asness C, Brown A; Social Science Research Network. Pulling the goalie: hockey and investment implications. https://ssrn.com/abstract=3132563. Published March 8, 2018. Updated October 8, 2018. Accessed May 29, 2019.

4. Haidt, J. *The Happiness Hypothesis: Finding Modern Truth in Ancient Wisdom*. New York, NY: Basic Books; 2006.

5. Unger JM, Cook E, Tai E, Bleyer A. The role of clinical trial participation in cancer research: barriers, evidence, and strategies. *ASCO Educ book*. 2016;36:185-198. doi:10.1200/EDBK_156686.

6. Tamblyn R, Eguale T, Huang A, Winslade N, Doran P. The incidence and determinants of primary nonadherence with prescribed medication in primary care. *Ann Intern Med*. 2014;160(7):441. doi:10.7326/M13-1705

7. Kahneman D. *Thinking, Fast and Slow*. New York, NY: Farrar, Straus, and Giroux; 2011.

8. Yaniv I, Benador D, Sagi M. On not wanting to know and not wanting to inform others: choices regarding predictive genetic testing. *Risk, Decis Policy*. 2004;9(4):317-336. doi:10.1080/14664530490896573.

9. Feltwell AK, Rees CE. The information-seeking behaviours of partners of men with prostate cancer: a qualitative pilot study. *Patient Educ Couns*. 2004;54(2):179-185. doi:10.1016/S0738-3991(03)00212-X.

10. Kerasidou A, Horn R. Making space for empathy: supporting doctors in the emotional labour of clinical care. *BMC Medical Ethics*. 2016;17(8). doi:10.1186/s12910-016-0091-7.

11. Busis NA, Shanafelt TD, Keran CM, et al. Burnout, career satisfaction, and well-being among US neurologists in 2016. *Neurology*. 2017;88(8):797-808. doi:10.1212/WNL.0000000000003640.

12. Kane L; Medscape. Medscape National Physician Burnout, Depression & Suicide Report 2019. https://www.medscape.com/slideshow/2019-lifestyle-burnout-depression-6011056. Published January 16, 2019. Assessed June 7, 2019.

13. Panagioti M, Geraghty K, Johnson J, et al. Association between physician burnout and patient safety, professionalism, and patient satisfaction: a systematic review and meta-analysis. *JAMA Intern Med*. 2018;178(10):1317-1330. doi:10.1001/jamainternmed.2018.3713.

14. Miller GA. The magical number seven, plus or minus two: some limits on our capacity for processing information. *Psychological Review*. 1956;63(2):81-97. https://psycnet.apa.org/doi/10.1037/h0043158. Assessed June 7, 2019.

15. Chernev A, Böckenholt U, Goodman J. Choice overload: A conceptual review and meta-analysis. 2015. doi:10.1016/j.jcps.2014.08.002.

16. Lengwiler Y. The origins of expected utility theory. In: *Vinzenz Bronzin's Option Pricing Models*. Berlin, Heidelberg: Springer Berlin Heidelberg; 2009:535-545. doi:10.1007/978-3-540-85711-2_26.

17. Tversky A, Kahneman D. The framing of decisions and the psychology of choice. *Science*. 1981;211(4481):453-458. doi:10.1126/science.7455683.

18. Bendahan S, Goette L, Thoresen J, Loued-Khenissi L, Hollis F, Sandi C. Acute stress alters individual risk taking in a time-dependent manner and leads to anti-social risk. *Eur J Neurosci*. 2017;45(7):877-885. doi:10.1111/ejn.13395.

19. Iyengar SS, Lepper MR. When choice is demotivating: can one desire too much of a good thing? *J Pers Soc Psychol*. 2000;79(6):995-1006. doi:10.1037/0022-3514.79.6.995.

20. Jachimowicz JM, Duncan S, Weber EU, Johnson EJ. When and why defaults influence decisions: a meta-analysis of default effects. *Behav Public Policy*. 2018;29:1-28. doi:10.1017/bpp.2018.43.

21. Madrian BC, Shea DF. The power of suggestion: Inertia in 401(k) participation and savings behavior. *Q J Econ*. 2001;116(4):1149-1187. doi:10.1162/003355301753265543.

22. Patel MS, Volpp KG, Asch DA. Nudge units to improve the delivery of health care. *N Engl J Med*. 2018;378(3):214-216. doi:10.1056/nejmp1712984.

23. Kuang, C. In the cafeteria, google gets healthy. Fast Company. https://www.fastcompany.com/1822516/cafeteria-google-gets-healthy. Published March 19, 2012. Assessed June 7, 2019.

24. Jachimowicz JM, Duncan S, Weber EU, Johnson EJ. When and why defaults influence decisions: a meta-analysis of default effects. *Behav Public Policy*. 2018;29:1-28. doi:10.1017/bpp.2018.43.

25. Soled D. The Ethics of Public Health Nudges: Libertarian Paternalism and the Manipulation of Choice [20th Annual Henry K. Beecher Prize in Medical Ethics]. Available at: https://bioethics.hms.harvard.edu/sites/g/files/mcu336/f/Derek Soled - Beecher Prize 2018.pdf. Published May 31, 2018. Accessed May 29, 2019.

26. Sunstein CR; Social Science Research Network. Nudging and choice architecture: ethical considerations [discussion paper no. 809]. http://ssrn.com/abstract=2551264. Updated January 23, 2015. Accessed May 29, 2019.

27. Groopman J, Hartzband P. Attribution error results from a positive stereotype. ACP Internist website. http://www.acpinternist.org/archives/2011/05/mindful.htm. Published May 2011. Accessed July 3, 2019.

28. van Empelen P, Kok G, Jansen MWJ, Hoebe CJPA. The additional value of anticipated regret and psychopathology in explaining intended condom use among drug users. *AIDS Care*. 2001;13(3):309-318. doi:10.1080/09540120120043964.

29. Abraham C, Sheeran P. Acting on intentions: the role of anticipated regret. *Br J Soc Psychol*. 2003;42(4):495-511. doi:10.1348/014466603322595248.

30. O'Carroll RE, Chambers JA, Brownlee L, Libby G, Steele RJC. Anticipated regret to increase uptake of colorectal cancer screening (ARTICS): a randomised controlled trial. *Soc Sci Med*. 2015;142:118-127. doi:10.1016/j.socscimed.2015.07.026.

31. Kolkey H. The Lung Cancer Project. Genentech website. https://www.gene.com/stories/the-lung-cancer-project. Published April 5, 2016. Accessed July 3, 2019.

32. Loewenstein G, Hagmann D, Schwartz J, et al; on behalf of the Behavioral Science & Policy Association Working Group on Health. Behavioral insights for health care policy. Carnegie Mellon University website. https://www.cmu.edu/dietrich/sds/docs/loewenstein/BehInsightsHealthCare.pdf. Accessed June 1, 2019.

33. Hupcey JE, Kitko L, Alonso W. Patients' perceptions of illness severity in advanced heart failure. *J Hosp Palliat Nurs*. 2016;18(2):110-114. doi:10.1097/NJH.0000000000000229.

34. Wolf L, Fiscella E, Cunningham H. 10 common errors healthcare professionals make communicating with their patients. *Nurse Educ*. 2008;33(6):237-240. doi:10.1097/01.NNE.0000334796.37923.c5.

35. Galanti GA. An introduction to cultural differences. *West J Med*. 2000;172(5):335-336. doi:10.1136/ewjm.172.5.335.

36. Crum AJ, Langer EJ. Mind-set matters: exercise and the placebo effect. *Psychol Sci*. 2007;18(2):165-171. doi:10.1111/j.1467-9280.2007.01867.x.

37. Householder L. Three creative nudges from Cannes. Syneos Health Communications website. https://syneoshealthcommunications.com/blog/three-creative-nudges-from-cannes. Published June 18, 2017. Accessed July 3, 2019.

38. Zahrt OH, Crum AJ. Perceived physical activity and mortality: evidence from three nationally representative U.S. samples. *Health Psychol*. 2017;36(11):1017-1025. doi:10.1037/hea0000531.supp.

39. Litt DM, Lewis MA, Linkenbach JW, Lande G, Neighbors C. Normative misperceptions of peer seat belt use among high school students and their relationship to personal seat belt use. *Traffic Inj Prev*. 2014;15(7):748-752. doi:10.1080/15389588.2013.868892.

40. Arbour-Nicitopoulos KP, Kwan MYW, Lowe D, Taman S, Faulkner GEJ. Social norms of alcohol, smoking, and marijuana use within a Canadian university setting. *J Am Coll Health*. 2010;59(3):191-196. doi:10.1080/07448481.2010.502194.

41. Suls JM, Davidson KW, Kaplan RM, eds. *Handbook of Health Psychology and Behavioral Medicine*. New York, NY: The Guilford Press; 2010.

42. Kessing D, Denollet J, Widdershoven J, Kupper N. Psychological determinants of heart failure self-care: systematic review and meta-analysis. *Psychosom Med*. 2016;78(4):412-431. doi:10.1097/PSY.0000000000000270.

43. Goldstein NJ, Cialdini RB, Griskevicius V. A room with a viewpoint: using social norms to motivate environmental conservation in hotels. *J Consum Res*. 2008;35:472-482. doi:10.1086/586910.

44. Anik L, Norton MI, Ariely D. Contingent match incentives increase donations. *J Mark Res*. 2014;51(6):790-801. doi:10.1509/jmr.13.0432.

45. Nair HS, Manchanda P, Bhatia T. Asymmetric social interactions in physician prescription behavior: the role of opinion leaders. *J Mark Res*. 2010;47(5):883-895. doi:10.1509/jmkr.47.5.883.

46. Heath D, Heath C. Why incentives are irresistible, effective, and likely to backfire. Fast Company website. https://www.fastcompany.com/1140924/why-incentives-are-irresistible-effective-and-likely-backfire. Published February 1, 2009. Accessed July 3, 2019.

47. Chatzisarantis NLD, Hagger MS, Wang JCK. Evaluating the effects of implementation intention and self-concordance on behaviour. *Br J Psychol*. 2010;101(Pt4):705-718. doi:10.1348/000712609X481796.

48. Sheeran P, Orbell S. Using implementation intentions to increase attendance for cervical cancer screening. *Health Psychol*. 2000;19(3):283-289. doi:10.1037/0278-6133.19.3.283.

49. Milkman KL, Beshears J, Choi JJ, Laibson D, Madrian BC. Using implementation intentions prompts to enhance influenza vaccination rates. *Proc Natl Acad Sci USA*. 2011;108(26):10415-10420. doi:10.1073/pnas.1103170108.

50. Milkman KL, Beshears J, Choi JJ, Laibson D, Madrian BC. Following through on good intentions: the power of planning prompts. The National Bureau of Economic Research website. http://www.nber.org/papers/w17995.ack. Accessed June 7, 2019.

51. Hortensius J, Kars MC, Wierenga WS, Kleefstra N, Bilo HJ, van der Bijl JJ. Perspectives of patients with type 1 or insulin-treated type 2 diabetes on self-monitoring of blood glucose: a qualitative study. *BMC Public Health*. 2012;12:167. doi:10.1186/1471-2458-12-167.

52. Kennedy L. Self-monitoring of blood glucose in type 2 diabetes: time for evidence of efficacy. *Diabetes Care*. 2001;24(6):977-978. doi:10.2337/diacare.24.6.977.

53. Gladwell M. *The Tipping Point : How Little Things Can Make a Big Difference*. Boston, MA: Back Bay Books; 2002.

54. Trafton A. *How the brain controls our habits*. MIT News website. http://news.mit.edu/2012/understanding-how-brains-control-our-habits-1029. Published October 29, 2012. Accessed July 3, 2019.

55. Duhigg C. *The Power of Habit : Why We Do What We Do in Life and Business*. New York, NY: Random House; 2012.

56. Lyubomirsky S. Hedonic adaptation to positive and negative experiences. In: Folkman S, ed. *The Oxford Handbook of Stress, Health, and Coping*. New York, NY: Oxford University Press; 2011:200-226.

57. Mochon D, Norton MI, Ariely D. Getting off the hedonic treadmill, one step at a time: the impact of regular religious practice and exercise on well-being. *J Econ Psychol*. 2008;29(5):632-642. doi:10.1016/j.joep.2007.10.004.

58. Dai H, Milkman KL, Riis J. The fresh start effect: temporal landmarks motivate aspirational behavior. *Manage Sci*. 2014;60(10):2563-2582. doi:10.1287/mnsc.2014.1901.

59. Hershfield HE. Future self-continuity: how conceptions of the future self transform intertemporal choice. *Ann N Y Acad Sci*. 2011;1235:30-43. doi:10.1111/j.1749-6632.2011.06201.x.

60. Gorman A. How are healthcare organizations making use of financial incentives to motivate patients? MedCity News website. https://medcitynews.com/2017/12/financial-incentives-to-boost-care-plan-adherence/. Published December 5, 2017. Accessed July 3, 2009.

61. Katch H, Solomon J. Restrictions on access to care don't improve Medicaid beneficiaries' health: incentives for healthy behaviors have mixed results. Center on Budget and Policy Priorities website. https://www.cbpp.org/research/health/restrictions-on-access-to-care-dont-improve-medicaid-beneficiaries-health. Updated December 11, 2018. Accessed July 3, 2019.

62. Hoerger T, Boland E, Kofi J, et al. Medicaid incentives for prevention of chronic diseases. Centers for Medicare & Medicaid Services website. https://downloads.cms.gov/files/cmmi/mipcd-finalevalrpt.pdf. Accessed July 3, 2019.

63. Higgins ET. Promotion and prevention: regulatory focus as a motivational principle. *Adv Exp Soc Psychol*. 1998;30:1-46. doi:10.1016/S0065-2601(08)60381-0.

64. Brodscholl JC, Kober H, Higgins ET. Strategies of self-regulation in goal attainment versus goal maintenance. *Eur J Soc Psychol*. 2007;37(4):628-648. doi:10.1002/ejsp.380.

65. Singelis TM. The measurement of independent and interdependent self-construals. *Personal Soc Psychol Bull*. 1994;20(5):580-591. doi:10.1177/0146167294205014.

66. Triandis HC, Bontempo R, Villareal MJ, Asai M, Lucca N. Individualism and collectivism: cross-cultural perspectives on self-ingroup relationships. *J Pers Soc Psychol*. 1988;54(2):323-338. doi:10.1037/0022-3514.54.2.323.

67. Oyserman D, Fryberg SA, Yoder N. Identity-based motivation and health. *J Pers Soc Psychol*. 2007;93(6):1011-1027. doi:10.1037/0022-3514.93.6.1011.

68. Sherman DK, Uskul AK, Updegraff JA. The role of the self in responses to health communications: a cultural perspective. *Self Identity*. 2011;10(3):284-294. doi:10.1080/15298868.2010.517029.

69. Kruglanski AW, Thompson EP, Higgins ET et al. To "do the right thing" or to "just do it": locomotion and assessment as distinct self-regulatory imperatives. *J Pers Soc Psychol*. 2000;79(5):793-815. doi:10.1037/0022-3514.79.5.793.

70. Higgins ET, Kruglanski AW, Pierro A. Regulatory mode: locomotion and assessment as distinct orientations. *Adv Exp Soc Psychol*. 2003;35:293-344. doi:10.1016/S0065-2601(03)01005-0.

71. Johnson S. How the "ghost map" helped end a killer disease. TED website. https://www.ted.com/talks/steven_johnson_tours_the_ghost_map?language=en. Accessed July 3, 2009.

72. Johnson S. The Ghost Map: The Story of London's Most Terrifying Epidemic—and How It Changed Science, Cities, and the Modern World. New York, NY: Riverhead Books; 2006.

Additional reading

Want more of the science behind the principles? Start with this curated list of just some of the fascinating research that informed the development of the principles.

Principle 1: Core Psychological Needs Drive Us

Andrade EB, Ariely D. The enduring impact of transient emotions on decision making. *Organ Behav Hum Decis Process*. 2009;109(1):1-8. doi:10.1016/j.obhdp.2009.02.003.

Baumeister RF, Leary MR. The need to belong: desire for interpersonal attachments as a fundamental human motivation. *Psychol Bull*. 1995;117(3):497-529.

Case DO, Andrews JE, Johnson JD, Allard SL. Avoiding versus seeking: the relationship of information seeking to avoidance, blunting, coping, dissonance, and related concepts. *J Med Libr Assoc*. 2005;93(3):353-362. http://www.pubmedcentral.nih.gov/articlerender.fcgi?artid=1175801&tool=pmcentrez&rendertype=abstract. Accessed June 7, 2019.

Dy SM, Purnell TS. Key concepts relevant to quality of complex and shared decision-making in health care: a literature review. *Soc Sci Med*. 2012;74(4):582-587. doi:10.1016/j.socscimed.2011.11.015.

Platonova EA, Shewchuk RM. Understanding patient satisfaction, trust, loyality to primary care physicians. *Med Care Res Rev*. 2008:696-712.

Ryan RM, Deci EL. Self-determination theory and the facilitation of intrinsic motivation, social development, and well-being. *Am Psychol*. 2000;55(1):68-78. http://www.ncbi.nlm.nih.gov/pubmed/11392867. Accessed June 7, 2019.

Ryan RM, Patrick H, Deci EL, Williams GC. Facilitating health behaviour change and its maintenance : interventions based on self-determination theory. *Eur Heal Psychol*. 2008;10:2-5.

Talevich JR, Read SJ, Walsh DA, Iyer R, Chopra G. Toward a comprehensive taxonomy of human motives. *PloS one*. 2017;12(2): e0172279. https://doi.org/10.1371/journal.pone.0172279. Published February 23, 2017. Accessed June 7, 2019.

Tay L, Diener E. Needs and subjective well-being around the world. *J Pers Soc Psychol*. 2011;101(2):354-365. doi:10.1037/a0023779.

Verlinde E, De Laender N, De Maesschalck S, Deveugele M, Willems S. The social gradient in doctor-patient communication. *Int J Equity Health*. 2012;11(1):12. doi:10.1186/1475-9276-11-12.

Visser PL, Hirsch JK. Health behaviors among college students: the influence of future time perspective and basic psychological need satisfaction. *Heal Psychol Behav Med*. 2014;2(1):88-99. doi:10.1080/21642850.2013.872992.

Wright LJ, Afari N, Zautra A. The illness uncertainty concept: a review. *Curr Pain Headache Rep*. 2009;13(2):133-138. doi:10.1007/s11916-009-0023-z.

Principle 2: Mental Processing is Limited

Beresford B, Sloper T. Social Policy Research Unit. Understanding the dynamics of decision-making and choice: a scoping study of key psychological theories to inform the design and analysis of the panel. https://www.york.ac.uk/inst/spru/pubs/pdf/decisionmaking.pdf. Published January 2008. Accessed June 7, 2019.

Burgess DJ. Are providers more likely to contribute to healthcare disparities under high levels of cognitive load? how features of the healthcare setting may lead to biases in medical decision making. *Med Decis Mak*. 2010;30(2):246-257. doi:10.1177/0272989X09341751.

Hough DE. *Irrationality in Health Care: What Behavioral Economics Reveals About What We Do and Why*. Stanford, CA: Stanford University Press; 2013.

Presseau J, Johnston M, Heponiemi T, et al. Reflective and automatic processes in health care professional behaviour: a dual process model tested across multiple behaviours. *Ann Behav Med*. 2014;48(3):347-358. doi:10.1007/s12160-014-9609-8.

Schaeffer MH. Environmental stress and individual decision-making: implications for the patient. *Patient Educ Couns*. 1989;13(3):221-235. doi:10.1016/0738-3991(89)90018-9.

Shevchenko Y, Helversen B Von, Scheibehenne B. Change and status quo in decisions with defaults: the effect of incidental emotions depends on the type of default. *Judgm Decis Mak*. 2014;9(3):287-296. http://journal.sjdm.org/13/13722/jdm13722.pdf. Accessed June 7, 2019.

Soares JM, Sampaio A, Ferreira LM, et al. Stress-induced changes in human decision-making are reversible. *Transl Psychiatry*. 2012;2(7):e131-e131. doi:10.1038/tp.2012.59.

Soled D; 20th Annual Henry K. Beecher Prize in Medical Ethics. The Ethics of Public Health Nudges: libertarian paternalism and the manipulation of choice. https://bioethics.hms.harvard.edu/sites/g/files/mcu336/f/Derek Soled - Beecher Prize 2018.pdf. Published May 31, 2018. Accessed May 29, 2019.

Starcke K, Brand M. Decision making under stress: a selective review. *Neurosci Biobehav Rev*. 2012;36(4):1228-1248. doi:10.1016/J.NEUBIOREV.2012.02.003.

Vohs K, Baumeister R, Twenge JM, Tice D. Making choices impairs subsequent self-control: a limited-resource account of decision making, self-regulation, and active initiative. *J Pers Soc Psychol*. 2008;94(5):883-898. doi:10.1037/0022-3514.94.5.883.

Principle 3: Irrational shortcuts guide decision making

Ariely D. *Predictably Irrational: The Hidden Forces That Shape Our Decisions*. New York, NY: HarperCollins; 2008.

Botti S, Iyengar SS. The psychological pleasure and pain of choosing: when people prefer choosing at the cost of subsequent outcome satisfaction. *J Pers Soc Psychol*. 2004;87(3):312-326. doi:10.1037/0022-3514.87.3.312.

Diamond P, Vartianen H. Behavioral Economics and Its Applications. Princeton, NJ: Princeton University Press; 2007.

Keller PA, Harlam B, Loewenstein G, Volpp KG. Enhanced active choice: a new method to motivate behavior change. *J Consum Psychol*. 2011;21(4):376-383. doi:10.1016/j.jcps.2011.06.003.

Mogler BK, Shu SB, Fox CR, et al. Using insights from behavioral economics and social psychology to help patients manage chronic diseases. *J Gen Intern Med*. 2013;28(5):711-718. doi:10.1007/s11606-012-2261-8.

Nease RF, Frazee SG, Zarin L, Miller SB. Choice architecture is a better strategy than engaging patients to spur behavior change. *Health Aff (Millwood)*. 2013;32(2):242-249. doi:10.1377/hlthaff.2012.1075.

Ferrer R, Klein W, Lerner J, Reyna V, Keltner D. Emotions and health decision- making: extending the appraisal tendency framework to improve health and healthcare. In: Roberto C, Kawachi I, ed. *Behavioral Economics and Public Health*. Oxford: Oxford University Press; 2016:101-131.

Samson, A. The behavioral economics guide 2018. Behavioraleconomics.com. 2018. https://www.behavioraleconomics.com/the-be-guide/the-behavioral-economics-guide-2018/. Accessed June 7, 2019.

Shevchenko Y, Helversen B Von, Scheibehenne B. Change and status quo in decisions with defaults: the effect of incidental emotions depends on the type of default. *Judgm Decis Mak*. 2014;9(3):287-296. http://journal.sjdm.org/13/13722/jdm13722.pdf. Accessed June 7, 2019.

Sunstein CR. Nudges that fail. *Behav Public Policy*. 2017;1(01):4-25. doi:10.1017/bpp.2016.3.

Tversky A, Kahneman D. Judgment under uncertainty: heuristics and biases. *Science*. 1974;185(4157):1124-1131. doi:10.1126/science.185.4157.1124.

Weinstein N, Klein W. Health risk appraisal and optimistic bias. In: Wright JD, ed. *International Encyclopedia of the Social and Behavioral Sciences*. 2nd ed. Amsterdam, Netherlands: Elsevier; 2015:698-701. https://doi.org/10.1016/B978-0-08-097086-8.25012-5. Published March 12, 2015. Accessed June 7, 2019.

Principle 4: We understand the present through the past

Abraham C, Michie S. A taxonomy of behavior change techniques used in interventions. *Psychol Assoc*. 2008;27(3):379-387. doi:10.1037/0278-6133.27.3.379.

Ambardekar AV, Thibodeau JT, DeVore AD, et al. Discordant perceptions of prognosis and treatment options between physicians and patients with advanced heart failure. *JACC Heart Fail*. 2017;5(9):663-671. doi:10.1016/j.jchf.2017.04.009.

Cacciatore MA, Scheufele DA, Iyengar S. The end of framing as we know it … and the future of media effects. *Mass Commun Soc*. 2016;19(1):7-23. doi:10.1080/15205436.2015.1068811.

de Hoog N, Stroebe W, de Wit JBF. The impact of vulnerability to and severity of a health risk on processing and acceptance of fear-arousing communications: a meta-analysis. *Rev Gen Psychol*. 2007;11(3):258-285. doi:10.1037/1089-2680.11.3.258.

Forgas JP. Mood and judgment: the affect infusion model (AIM). *Psychol Bull*. 1995;117(1):39-66. doi:10.1037//0033-2909.117.1.39.

FrameWorks Institute. Framing Public Issues. http://www.frameworksinstitute.org/assets/files/PDF/FramingPublicIssuesfinal.pdf. Updated June 2004. Accessed June 7, 2019.

Garcia-Retamero R, Hoffrage, U. Visual representation of statistical information improves diagnostic inferences in doctors and their patients. In: Kawachi I, ed. *Social Science and Medicine*; vol 83. Amsterdam, Netherlands: Elsevier; 2013:27-33. https://doi.org/10.1016/j.socscimed.2013.01.034. Published February 8, 2013. Accessed June 7, 2019.

Gobet F, Lane PCR, Croker S, et al. Chunking mechanisms in human learning. *Trends Cogn Sci*. 2001;5(6):236-243. doi:10.1016/S1364-6613(00)01662-4.

Hooper N, Erdogan A, Keen G, Lawton K, McHugh L. Perspective taking reduces the fundamental attribution error. *J Context Behav Sci*. 2015;4(2):69-72. doi:10.1016/J.JCBS.2015.02.002

Horne R, Graupner L, Frost S, Weinman J, Wright SM, Hankins M. Medicine in a multi-cultural society: the effect of cultural background on beliefs about medications. In: Kawachi I, ed. *Social Science and Medicine*; vol 59(6). Amsterdam, Netherlands: Elsevier; 2004: 1307-1313. https://doi.org/10.1016/j.socscimed.2004.01.009. Published March 14, 2004. Accessed June 7, 2019.

Le Pelley ME, Mitchell CJ, Beesley T, George DN, Wills AJ. Attention and associative learning in humans: an integrative review. *Psychol Bull*. 2016;142(10):1111-1140. doi:10.1037/bul0000064.

O'Keefe DJ, Jensen JD. The relative persuasiveness of gain-framed and loss-framed messages for encouraging disease detection behaviors: a meta-analytic review. *J Commun*. 2009;59(2):296-316. doi:10.1111/j.1460-2466.2009.01417.x.

Phillips LA, Leventhal EA, Leventhal H. Factors associated with the accuracy of physicians' predictions of patient adherence. *Patient Educ Couns*. 2011;85(3):461-467.

Renner B, Gamp M, Schmalze R, Schupp HT. Health risk perception. In: Wright JD, ed. *International Encyclopedia of the Social and Behavioral Sciences*. 2nd ed. Amsterdam, Netherlands: Elsevier; 2015 702-709. doi:10.1016/B978-0-08-097086-8.14138-8.

Weiner B. Attribution theory. In: Peterson P, Baker E, McGraw B, ed. *International Encyclopedia of Education*. 3rd ed. Amsterdam Netherlands: Elsevier: 2010: 558-563. https://doi.org/10.1016/B978-0-08-044894-7.00600-X. Published May 26, 2010. Accessed June 7, 2019.

Principle 5: Self as a social phenomenon

Allcott H. Social norms and energy conservation. *J Public Econ*. 2011;95(9-10):1082-1095. doi:10.1016/J.JPUBECO.2011.03.003

Bandura A. Human Agency in Social Cognitive Theory. *Am Psychol*. 1989;44(9):1175-1184.

Donohue JM, Guclu H, Gellad WF, et al. Influence of peer networks on physician adoption of new drugs. *PLoS One*. 2018;13(10): e0204826. doi:10.1371/journal.pone.0204826.

Fogg B. A Behavior model for persuasive design. In: Proceedings of the 4th International Conference on Persuasive Technology - Persuasive '09. New York, NY: ACM; 2009:40:1-40:7.

Gillespie AMH, Johnson-Askew WL. Changing family food and eating practices: the family food decision-making system. *Ann Behav Med*. 2009;38(suppl 1):S31-6. doi:10.1007/s12160-009-9122-7.

Heisler M; California Healthcare Foundation. Building peer support programs to manage chronic disease: seven models for success. https://www.chcf.org/wp-content/uploads/2017/12/PDF-BuildingPeerSupportPrograms.pdf. Published December 2006. Accessed June 7, 2019.

Hornsey MJ. Social identity theory and self-categorization theory: a historical review. *Soc Personal Psychol Compass*. 2008;2(1):204-222. doi:10.1111/j.1751-9004.2007.00066.x.

Oyserman D, Fryberg SA, Yoder N. Identity-based motivation and health. *J Pers Soc Psychol*. 2007;93(6):1011-1027.

Rogers A, Vassilev I, Sanders C, et al. Social networks, work and network-based resources for the management of long-term conditions: a framework and study protocol for developing self-care support. *Implement Sci*. 2011;6(1):56. doi:10.1186/1748-5908-6-56.

Rogers EM. *Diffusion of Innovations*. 5th ed. New York, NY: Free Press; 2003.

Shepperd JA, Rothman AJ, Klein WMP. Using self- and identity-regulation to promote health: promises and challenges. *Self Identity*. 2011;10(3):407-416. doi:10.1080/15298868.2011.577198.

Principle 6: Goals organize our behavior

Gutnick D, Reims K, Davis C, Gainforth H, Jay M, Cole S. Brief action planning to facilitate behavior change and support patient self-management. *J Clin Outcomes Manag*. 2014;18(1):17-29.

Höchli B, Brügger A, Messner C. How focusing on superordinate goals motivates broad, long-term goal pursuit: A theoretical perspective. *Front Psychol*. 2018;9:1-14. doi:10.3389/fpsyg.2018.01879.

Kluger AN, Denisi AS. The effects of feedback interventions on performance: a historical review, a meta-analysis, and a preliminary feedback intervention theory. *Psychol Bull*. 1996;119(2):254-284. doi:10.1037/0033-2909.119.2.254.

Locke EA, Latham GP. Building a practically useful theory of goal setting and task motivation: a 35-year odyssey. *Am Psychol*. 2002;57(9):705-717. doi:10.1037/0003-066X.57.9.705.

Miltenberger RG. Behavioral Modification: Principles and Procedures. 5th ed. Belmont, CA: Wadsworth Cengage Learning; 2012.

Oettingen G, Bulgarella C, Henderson M, Gollwitzer PM. The self-regulation of goal pursuit. In: Wright RA, Greenberg J, Brehm SS, ed. *Motivational Analyses of Social Behavior: Building on Jack Brehm's Contributions to Psychology*. Mahwah, NJ: Lawrence Erlbaum Associates; 2002:225-244. https://pdfs.semanticscholar.org/9e1f/0593612c43051973d901f9e4ce6015214288.pdf. Accessed June 7, 2019.

Sullivan HW, Rothman AJ. When planning is needed: implementation intentions and attainment of approach versus avoidance health goals. *Health Psychol*. 2008;27(4):438-444. doi:10.1037/0278-6133.27.4.438.

Vohs KD, Baumeister RF, ed. *Handbook of Self Regulation*. 2nd ed. New York, NY: The Guilford Press; 2013.

Wrosch C, Scheier MF, Miller GE, Schulz R, Carver CS. Adaptive self-regulation of unattainable goals: goal disengagement, goal reengagement, and subjective well-being. *Pers Soc Psychol Bull*. 2003;29(12):1494-1508. doi:10.1177/0146167203256921.

Principle 7: Context is critical to our habits

Burns RJ, Rothman AJ. Offering variety: a subtle manipulation to promote healthy food choice throughout the day. *Health Psychol*. 2015;34(5):566-570. doi:10.1037/hea0000164.

Dijksterhuis A, van Knippenberg A, Holland RW. Evaluating behavior priming research: three observations and a recommendation. *Social Cognition*. 2014;32(suppl):196-208. doi:10.1521/soco.2014.32.supp.196

Fogg B. A Behavior model for persuasive design. In: Proceedings of the 4th International Conference on Persuasive Technology - Persuasive '09. New York, NY: ACM; 2009:40:1-40:7.

Lally P, Gardner B. Promoting habit formation. *Health Psychol Rev*. 2013;7(supp1):S137-S158. doi:10.1080/17437199.2011.603640.

Miltenberger RG. *Behavioral Modification: Principles and Procedures*. 5th ed. Belmont, CA: Wadsworth Cengage Learning; 2012.

Neal DT, Wood W, Labrecque JS, Lally P. How do habits guide behavior? Perceived and actual triggers of habits in daily life. *J Exp Soc Psychol*. 2012;48(2):492-498. doi:10.1016/J.JESP.2011.10.011.

Ouellette JA, Wood W, Aizen I, et al. Habit and intention in everyday life: the multiple processes by which past behavior predicts future behavior. *Psychol Bull*. 1998;124(1):54-74.

Papies EK. Situating interventions to bridge the intention–behaviour gap: a framework for recruiting nonconscious processes for behaviour change. *Soc Personal Psychol Compass*. 2017;11(7):1-19. doi:10.1111/spc3.12323.

Principle 8: We constantly redefine normal

Borland R. CEOS theory: a comprehensive approach to understanding hard to maintain behaviour change. In: *Applied Phychology: Health and Well-Being*. Indianapolis, IN: John Wiley and Sons; 2017:9(1):3-35. doi:10.1111/aphw.12083.

Brickman P, Coates D, Janoff-Bulman R. Lottery winners and accident victims: is happiness relative? *J Pers Soc Psychol*. 1978;36(8):917-927.

Carver CS, Scheier MF. Control theory: a useful conceptual framework for personality-social, clinical, and health psychology. *Psychol Bull*. 1982;92(1):111-135.

Coyne JC, Tennen H, Ranchor AV. Positive psychology in cancer care: a story line resistant to evidence. *Ann Behav Med*. 2010;39(1):35-42. doi:10.1007/s12160-010-9157-9.

Ferrer R, Klein W, Lerner J, Reyna V, Keltner D. Emotions and health decision- making: extending the appraisal tendency framework to improve health and healthcare. In: Roberto C, Kawachi I, ed. *Behavioral Economics and Public Health*. Oxford: Oxford University Press; 2016:101-131.

Fletcher D, Sarkar M. Psychological resilience. *Eur Psychol*. 2013;18(1):12-23. doi:10.1027/1016-9040/a000124.

Marlatt GA, George WH. Relapse prevention: introduction and overview of the model. *Addiction*. 1984;79(4):261-273. doi:10.1111/j.1360-0443.1984.tb03867.x.

Matuz T, Birbaumer N, Hautzinger M, Kübler A. Psychosocial adjustment to ALS: a longitudinal study. *Front Psychol*. 2015;6:1-12. doi:10.3389/fpsyg.2015.01197.

Zajonc RB. Mere exposure: a gateway to the subliminal. *Curr Dir Psychol Sci*. 2001;10(6):224-228. doi:10.1111/1467-8721.00154.

Principle 9: Motivation is Fleeting

Bandura A. Self-efficacy. In: Ramachaudran VS, ed. *Encyclopedia of Human Behavior*. Academic Press (Reprinted in H. Friedman [Ed.], Encyclopedia of mental health. San Diego: Academic Press, 1998); 1994:71-81.

Baumeister RE, Bratslavsky E, Muraven M, Tice DM. Ego depletion: is the active self a limited resource? *J Pers Soc Psychol*. 1998;24(5):1252-1265.

Davies MJ, Gagliardino JJ, Gray LJ, Khunti K, Mohan V, Hughes R. Real-world factors affecting adherence to insulin therapy in patients with type 1 or type 2 diabetes mellitus: a systematic review. *Diabet Med*. 2013;30(5):512-524. doi:10.1111/dme.12128.

Dusseldorp E, van Genugten L, van Buuren S, Verheijden MW, van Empelen P. Combinations of techniques that effectively change health behavior: evidence from meta-CART analysis. *Health Psychol*. 2014;33(12):1530-1540. http://dx.doi.org/10.1037/hea0000018.

Gneezy U, Meier S, Rey-Biel P. When and why incentives (don't) work to modify behavior. *J Econ Perspect*. 2011;25(4):191-210. doi:10.1257/jep.25.4.191.

Michie S, van Stralen MM, West R. The behaviour change wheel: a new method for characterising and designing behaviour change interventions. *Implement Sci*. 2011;6(1):42. doi:10.1186/1748-5908-6-42.

Rothman AJ, Sheeran P, Wood W. Reflective and automatic processes in the initiation and maintenance of dietary change. *Ann Behav Med*. 2009;38 Suppl 1:S4-17. doi:10.1007/s12160-009-9118-3.

Ryan RM, Deci EL. Intrinsic and extrinsic motivations: classic definitions and new directions. *Contemp Educ Psychol.* 2000;25(1):54-67. doi:10.1006/CEPS.1999.1020.

Silva Castillo LH. Temporal discounting and health behavior: a review. *MOJ Public Heal.* 2018;6(6). doi:10.15406/mojph.2017.06.00189.

Simpson CA, Vuchinch RE. Temporal changes in the value of objects of choice: discounting, behavior patterns, and health behavior. In: Bickel WK, Vuchinich RE, ed. *Reframing Health Behavior Change with Behavioral Economics.* Mahwah, NJ: Lawrence Erlbaum Associates; 2000:417.

Trudel R, Murray KB. Self-regulatory strength amplification through selective information processing. *J Consum Psychol.* 2013;23(1):61-73. doi:10.1016/j.jcps.2012.02.002.

Vohs KD, Baumeister RF, ed. *Handbook of Self Regulation.* 2nd ed. New York, NY: The Guilford Press; 2013.

Part 2: The (Behavioral) Science of Segmenting

Avnet T, Laufer D, Higgins ET. Are all experiences of fit created equal? Two paths to persuasion. *J Consum Psychol.* 2013;23(3):301-316. doi:10.1016/j.jcps.2012.10.011.

Clark M, Ouellette R, Powell M, Milberg S. Communal orientation scale (Cos). *J Pers Soc Psychol.* 1987;53:94-103.

Fuglestad PT, Rothman AJ, Jeffery RW. The effects of regulatory focus on responding to and avoiding slips in a longitudinal study of smoking cessation. *Basic Appl Soc Psych.* 2013;35(5):426-435. doi:10.1080/01973533.2013.823619.

Gomez P, Borges A, Pechmann C. Avoiding poor health or approaching good health: does it matter? The conceptualization, measurement, and consequences of health regulatory focus. *J Consum Psychol.* 2013;23(4):451-463. doi:10.1016/j.jcps.2013.02.001.

Higgins ET. Value from regulatory fit. *Curr Dir Psychol Sci.* 2005;14(4):209-213. doi:10.1111/j.0963-7214.2005.00366.x.

Triandis HC, Gelfand MJ. Converging measurement of horizontal and vertical individualism and collectivism. *J Pers Soc Psychol.* 1998;74(1):118-128.

About the Authors

Kathleen

Kathleen R. Starr, Ph.D.

Kathleen is one of the great teachers of our industry. She has been a professor, a clinician, a business leader, and now a leading voice for how behavioral science can fuel more powerful, effective healthcare communications and education. Kathleen has developed behavioral interventions with some of the leading brands in healthcare and is working to innovate omnichannel communication programs leveraging behavioral segmentation. She's learned about people 1:1 as a practicing psychologist and now scales that knowledge through research and ethnography programs that seek to understand the everyday challenges, barriers, and joys of life and health.

Leigh Householder

Leigh began her career creating digital, social and loyalty strategies for Fortune 1000 brands. Ten years ago, she made the move to healthcare and never looked back. Leigh was a strategic lead on one of medicine's biggest launches and has been an important partner to brands working to improve the lives of people fighting both chronic and acute diseases. Today, she invests a lot of her time interviewing and engaging people who work on the frontlines of healthcare around the world to both understand and prioritize the shifts changing the industry and the world. You can see her annual compilation of leading life science trends at trends.health

CPSIA information can be obtained
at www.ICGtesting.com
Printed in the USA
LVHW051200190820
663573LV00007B/264